T0094750

"Yogi Was Up with a Guy on Third..."

"Yogi Was Up with a Guy on Third..."

Hall of Famers Recall Their Favorite Baseball Games Ever

Maureen Mullen

TRIUMPH
B O O K S

Library of Congress Cataloging-in-Publication Data

Mullen, Maureen, 1963–
  Yogi was up with a guy on third : Hall of Famers recall their favorite baseball games ever / Maureen Mullen.
       p. cm.
  ISBN 978-1-60078-162-9
  1. Baseball—United States—History. 2. Baseball players—United States—Anecdotes. I. Title.
  GV863.A1M85 2009
  796.357'640973—dc22

                                                    2008050253

This book is available in quantåity at special discounts for your group or organization. For further information, contact:

Triumph Books
542 South Dearborn Street
Suite 750
Chicago, Illinois 60605
(312) 939-3330
Fax (312) 663-3557

Printed in USA
ISBN: 978-1-60078-162-9
Design by Patricia Frey
All photos courtesy of AP Images unless otherwise indicated

For Ryan, Chris, Meagan, Connor, Danny, Jack, Timmy, and Cecelia, and hoping there are many favorite memories ahead for you.

Contents

by order of induction into the Hall of Fame

Foreword

Growing up in Cuba, baseball was all we had. Baseball and boxing. There was no soccer, no volleyball, no tennis. Just baseball. We played every day. My father played in Cuba and in the Negro Leagues. He was a pitcher, and he taught me how to pitch. Baseball was everything and was very important to my family. It was a way to a better life, and it was all I wanted to do.

When I made my major-league debut, I wasn't really nervous because I knew what I could do. I spent five and a half years in the minor leagues. I worked at it. I thank God that He gave me the personality to be tough. I wasn't afraid of anybody. I don't mean that I wanted to fight people, but I was not afraid to pitch to anybody. I believed in myself and knew what I could do. That's the key to anything in life: you have to believe in yourself. But, you have to work at your talents, too. I wasn't going to listen to anybody tell me what I could or couldn't do. I knew what I could do. If you give me a chance, I know what I can do. God gives different chances to different people. It might not be in baseball; it might be something else. But you have to take advantage of that. Don't listen to other people tell you what you can or can't do. You have to find that drive inside of yourself. You can't rely on other people to motivate you; you have to motivate yourself. You have to know who you are and what you want to be, and you have to work for it. You might not get there, but at least you'll know you worked for it and you tried.

I got hurt a couple of times, but I came back. I won more games after I got hurt than before. Not everybody can do that, but that's what I wanted to do. You have to keep working for what you want.

When I finally made it to the major leagues, I fulfilled my dreams. God fulfilled my dreams. I know how fortunate I was, because not many people can say that. I had a wonderful career and great teammates and friends. I accomplished a lot in baseball. I can die tomorrow a happy man; I have nothing to regret or wish I had done differently. I did what I wanted to do. For me, that's a marvelous thing that a human can do that and live that kind of life. I wish everyone could do that.

I think of my first game and my last game. I pitched 19 years and was very lucky to be able to do that. I had a wonderful career. I was never jealous of what anyone else had or if someone had something I didn't have. I never cared what anybody had. I just wanted to live in my own little world. I made a good living with what I had. I have been very lucky, very blessed, and very happy. Baseball gave me that.

—Luis Tiant

Acknowledgments

As I was working on this project, I was asked many questions about its genesis. The short answer is, I'm not exactly sure. I think it partially evolved from conversations with family and friends about the "glory days" and "Remember when..." and "How about that time...".

And then I got to wondering if professional athletes have one game from their careers or lives that they can pinpoint as their favorite. That thought progressed to wondering if Hall of Famers—with the obviously impressive careers they each had—are able to pick one favorite game.

In talking with the subjects of this book, I was surprised at how many of them—a huge majority—really didn't have to think about the question very long to come up with a favorite game. I simply asked them for one favorite game or one game that stands out in their memories. It didn't necessarily have to be the biggest or best game they ever played, although it could be. For many of them, I had barely finished the question before they had a response ready. While I asked for one particular game, a few of the subjects had more than one they wanted to include. So I figured, well, who am I to tell a Hall of Famer he can only choose one game?

When I started working on this project, there were 64 living Hall of Famers—63 players/managers and one executive—including the 2008 inductees. My goal was to include all 64 in this book. Unfortunately, for various reasons, I was only able to get 53. But I figure that's a success rate of .828, which, in baseball terms, is pretty good.

Players can gain election to the National Baseball Hall of Fame in one of two ways. First, qualified members of the Baseball Writers' Association of American (BBWAA) can vote on players who have played at least 10 years and have been retired for at least five years. If an active player or a player who has been retired for less than five years dies but is otherwise qualified, he becomes eligible for the next vote at least six months later. Also, the Veterans Committee votes on players whose careers ended at least 21 seasons ago, along with managers, umpires, and executives. A candidate who receives votes on at least 75 percent of the ballots cast gains election to the Hall of Fame.

I could not have completed a project of this size without a great deal of help from many people. I would like to thank all of them and only hope I don't leave anyone out. So, here goes.

First, thanks to my family for their continuous support and encouragement—Jack Mullen, Bob and Cyndi Mullen, Janet and Charlie Ehl, Kevin and Amy Mullen, Jane and Henry Gioacchini, Elaine and Michael Kuzmin, and Terry Mullen.

And, of course, to the Hall of Famers for generously sharing their memories with me—Hank Aaron, Sparky Anderson, Luis Aparicio, Yogi Berra, Wade Boggs, George Brett, Lou Brock, Rod Carew, Gary Carter, Orlando Cepeda, Bobby Doerr, Dennis Eckersley, Ernie Banks, Bob Feller, Rollie Fingers, Carlton Fisk, Whitey Ford, Rich Gossage, Tony Gwynn, Monte Irvin, Reggie Jackson,

Ferguson Jenkins, Al Kaline, George Kell, Harmon Killebrew, Ralph Kiner, Tommy Lasorda, Lee MacPhail Jr., Juan Marichal, Bill Mazeroski, Willie McCovey, Paul Molitor, Joe Morgan, Eddie Murray, Phil Niekro, Jim Palmer, Tony Perez, Gaylord Perry, Cal Ripken Jr., Robin Roberts, Brooks Robinson, Nolan Ryan, Ryne Sandberg, Mike Schmidt, Red Schoendienst, Ozzie Smith, Bruce Sutter, Earl Weaver, Dick Williams, Billy Williams, Dave Winfield, Carl Yastrzemski, and Robin Yount.

Friends and colleagues provided immense help and support throughout the process, including Loretta Andreattola; Ron Antonucci; Freddy Berowski; John Blake; Barry Bloom; John Boggs; Dick Bresciani; Brian Bartow; Brian Britten; Rob Butcher; Nick Cafardo; Peter Chase; Joe Christensen; Abby DeCiccio; Matt Deutschman; Marcia Dick; Ray Doswell; Dawn-Marie Driscoll; Sgt. Rory Duane; Bill Dunstone; Tom Eckel; Liz Ellze; Elena Elms; friends, colleagues, and coworkers at Fenway Park; Nick Frankovich; Pam Ganley; Dick Gordon; Paul Hagen; Brad Hainje; Eric Ham; Fran Healy; Anne Heffernan; Roland Hemond; Diane Hock; Brad Horn; Rick Hummel; Jeff Idelson; Paul Jensen; Dick Johnson; Ron Kaplan; Steve Krasner; Steve Krause; Mark Langill; Henry Mahegan; Norman Marcus; Debbie Matson; Rob Matwick; Robert "Skip" McAfee; Hal McCoy; Andy McCue; Erin McDonald; Sarah McKenna; John McMurray; Phyllis Merhige; Rob Metwick; Craig Muder; Rod Nelson; Bill Nowlin; Jack O'Connell; Sally O'Leary; Mark Pankin; Peter Pascarelli; Mark Rogoff; Bill Shaikin; Larry Shenk; Jon Shestakofsky; Bill Simons; Tom Singer; Lyle Spatz; Steve Steinberg; Bill Stetka; Jim Stimac; T.R. Sullivan; Bart Swain; Mike Swanson; Luis Tiant; Luis Tiant Jr.; Jim Trdinich; Triumph Books' Tom Bast, Don

Gulbrandsen, and Laine Morreau; David Vincent; Jabin White; John Zajc; Jason Zillo and Gene Zonarich.

Invaluable assistance and resource information was provided by the National Baseball Hall of Fame, the Negro Leagues Baseball Museum, Baseball-almanac. com, BaseballLibrary.com, Baseball-reference.com, Major League Baseball and each team's media guide produced by the media-relations departments, MLB.com, Retrosheet. org, the Society for American Baseball Research, and TheBaseballPage.com. The Hall of Fame served as the primary source for statistics and information and others were used as secondary sources.

And now I hope you enjoy reading this book as much as I enjoyed working on it.

—M.A.M.

Bob Feller

Robert William Andrew Feller
Born: November 3, 1918, in Van Meter, Iowa
MLB debut: July 19, 1936
Final game: September 30, 1956
Team: Cleveland Indians (1936–1941, 1945–1956)
Primary position: Pitcher
Bats: Right—**Throws:** Right
Hall of Fame induction: 1962
Vote: 150 of 160 ballots cast, 93.75%

After pitching for the Indians for six seasons and establishing his blazing fastball as the gold standard, on December 8, 1941, Bob Feller became one of the first ballplayers to enlist in the service, giving up nearly four full seasons to serve in the navy during World War II. He earned five campaign ribbons and eight battle stars.

Known as "Rapid Robert" and the "Heater from Van Meter," Feller returned at the end of the 1945 season and the following year appeared in an American League–high 48 games—one of three seasons he led the league in appearances—starting 42 with 36 complete games and 10 shutouts, and going 26–15 with a 2.18 ERA, 348 strikeouts, and 153 walks in 371 innings.

As a 17-year-old right out of high school, Feller struck out 17 Athletics in one game in his rookie year of 1936. He became the first pitcher to win 20 or more games in a season before the age of 21, going 24–9 in 1939 at the age of 20.

He had already won 31 games before he turned 20. He led the American League in wins six times and in strikeouts seven times. An eight-time All-Star, in 1940 the right-hander won the AL pitching Triple Crown, with a record of 27–11, an ERA of 2.62, and 261 strikeouts. He was also named the Major League Player of the Year that season.

Feller went on to an 18-year career, with 266 wins against 162 losses, for a .621 winning percentage with a 3.25 ERA. In 3,828 career innings he had 2,581 strikeouts against 1,764 walks. In 1999 he was ranked No. 36 on *The Sporting News* list of 100 Greatest Baseball Players.

While he shares the record for one-hitters with 12, Feller threw three no-hitters, including the only Opening Day no-no, on April 16, 1940, winning 1–0 against the White Sox; July 1, 1951, in the first game of a doubleheader against the Tigers; and no-hitting the Yankees for the first time in almost 27 years.

My favorite game was the no-hitter in Yankee Stadium on April 30, 1946, 1–0. Neither team was going anywhere. The Yankees finished far behind. We were in sixth place. The Red Sox won it going away, then lost the World Series in seven to the St. Louis Cardinals.

That was my favorite ballgame. I had just come out of the service after spending four years in the United States Navy. That was not my first game back. I pitched in September 1945 when I was on inactive duty in the navy. That's when we concluded the war in the Pacific and the war was over.

I was in very good condition, and '46 was my best year. I got the win in the All-Star Game in Fenway Park in

Cleveland Indians pitcher Bob Feller was one the greatest fastball pitchers in baseball. Here, Feller pitches in the 1948 World Series against the Boston Braves.

'46. And that was my best game in Yankee Stadium, the no-hitter. I had very good stuff, struck out 11. I don't recall if I shook off the catcher or not. Probably not. Frankie Hayes was very good at calling pitches. He hit a home run in the ninth inning with one man out. That's the only run in that ballgame. That was the first no-hitter pitched against the Yankees since 1919.

DiMaggio was my toughest out. He grounded out to shortstop with the tying run on second base, Snuffy Stirnweiss, he went to third base on that play. And when Charlie Keller grounded out for the final out, the tying run was on third base. And that was the largest crowd to see a no-hitter up until that date in time, almost 40,000. But Charlie Keller hit a nice ground ball to my second baseman, Ray Mack, who also made the last out of my Opening Day no-hitter in 1940 in Chicago.

It's difficult to believe how much time has gone by. It seems like it was just yesterday that it all happened, and you try to remember everything. Of course, you forget a lot of things and you have to have your memory refreshed. But I'm very proud of the fact that I'm still around to talk about my career and help the game of baseball if I can do so. It helped me a lot. Anything I may be today is due to what baseball has done for me.

Yogi Berra

Lawrence Peter Berra
Born: May 12, 1925, in St. Louis, Missouri
MLB debut: September 22, 1946
Final game: May 9, 1965
Teams: New York Yankees (1946–1963), New York Mets (1965)
Primary position: Catcher
Bats: Left—**Throws:** Right
Hall of Fame induction: 1972
Vote: 339 of 396 ballots cast, 85.61%

More than 40 years after his playing career ended, Yogi Berra remains one of the most popular figures in baseball. In his 19-year playing career, he was named to the American League All-Star team in 15 consecutive seasons, from 1948 to 1962, and was named the AL's MVP three times: 1951, 1954, and 1955. He had over 100 RBIs five times, including in four straight seasons from 1953 to 1956.

Yogi played on more World Series–winning teams (10) and pennant winners (14) than any other player in baseball history. Yogi holds the World Series record for appearances (14), games (75), at-bats (259), hits (71), doubles (10), singles (49), games caught (63), and catcher putouts (421).

At the plate, Yogi was known for both his bat control and bat speed. In five seasons, he had more home runs than strikeouts. In 1950 he had just 12 strikeouts, compared to 28 home runs in 597 at-bats. In 2,120 career games, Yogi hit .285 with 358 home runs and 1,430 RBIs.

Behind the plate, Yogi was known for his agility and ability to work with pitchers. He led AL catchers in games caught in eight seasons, six times in double plays, eight times in putouts, three times in assists, and once in fielding percentage. In 1958 he had a perfect 1.000 fielding percentage behind the plate, committing no errors in 88 games, 755 innings. He caught a then-record 148 consecutive games without committing an error.

In 1999 he was named to MLB's All-Century Team and ranked No. 40 on *The Sporting News* list of 100 Greatest Baseball Players.

Of course, Yogi is known for his "Yogi-isms," witty comments and malaprops that concisely capture a moment or thought, of which he once said, "I never said half the things I really said."

Yogi's playing days ended with the 1963 World Series, except for four games with the Mets in 1965. He went on to coach and manage. As a manager Yogi led the Yankees to the 1964 World Series and the Mets to the 1973 World Series and won the 1969 World Series with the Mets as a coach.

But, for all his accomplishments, it is one particular October afternoon when he was behind the plate that stands out for Yogi.

The no-hitter that Larsen pitched in '56 [the perfect game in Game 5 of the 1956 World Series, the only no-hitter ever pitched in the postseason]. It's never happened before. It was one of my biggest thrills, besides getting into the Hall of Fame. The Hall of Fame was a big thrill, too.

He had good control. That's what he had. Anything I put down, he got over. He pitched to good spots. He

New York Yankees manager Casey Stengel, left, shakes hands with Yankees record-breaking catcher Yogi Berra as they celebrate the 1956 World Series victory in their dressing room after the deciding game against the Brooklyn Dodgers at Ebbets Field on October 10.

only went to three balls on one hitter. That was in the first inning to Pee Wee Reese. He only threw 97 pitches [71 for strikes].

I didn't warm him up. But you never know. Some guys have good stuff in the bullpen and come in the game and not have good stuff. But he had good stuff that day. He threw hard. Of course, he pitched the second game [of the 1956 World Series]. We gave him a six-run lead and we lost. And then he came back and pitched a no-hitter. He really came back. But anything you put down, he had good control. Pitched to his spots.

All his pitches were great that day. Anything I put down, he got it over. Fastballs, sliders, everything. We didn't want to say anything to him, especially late in the game. But we knew what was going on. But we didn't think we had a safe lead. It was only 2–0. We were saying, "C'mon, let's go get a few more runs." You know, they get one guy on and then the tying run comes up. But all his pitches were great. That last pitch, it was right on the corner. It wasn't high at all.

I love this game. I really do. But yeah, that was my favorite.

How did I celebrate? I guess I went home and ate dinner.

Monte Irvin

Monford Merrill Irvin
Born: February 25, 1919, in Columbia, Alabama
MLB debut: July 8, 1949
Final game: September 30, 1956
Teams: Newark Eagles (1937–1942, 1945–1948), New York
    Giants (1949–1955), Chicago Cubs (1956)
Primary position: Left field
Bats: Right—**Throws:** Right
Hall of Fame induction: 1973
Vote: Elected to the Hall of Fame by the Negro Leagues
    Committee

Monte Irvin began playing in the Negro Leagues as a teenager
with the Newark Eagles in 1937 as "Jimmy Nelson" to maintain
his amateur status while at East Orange (New Jersey) High
School and later at Lincoln University in Pennsylvania. He
won Negro Leagues batting titles in 1941 with a .395 average
and in 1946 with a .404 mark.

A contract dispute with Eagles owner Effa Manley in 1942
sent him to the Mexican League for a short time. In 63 games
with the Vera Cruz team, Irvin led the league in batting (with a
.397 clip) and home runs (with 20) and was second in RBIs
(with 79), earning MVP honors.

After returning from the army during World War II he led the
Eagles to the pennant in 1946, capturing his second batting
title, and then to a Negro League World Series championship,
hitting .462 with three home runs against the Kansas City

Monarchs. He was a five-time Negro League All-Star, playing in four Negro League All-Star Games, in 1941, 1946, 1947, and 1948.

Irvin was said to be the choice of Negro League team owners to be the player who would break Major League Baseball's color barrier, but while Irvin was in the service, Branch Rickey chose Jackie Robinson. Irvin was originally signed by the Dodgers, but Eagles owner Manley and the Dodgers could not reach an agreement on compensation. The Dodgers then withdrew their claim, allowing the New York Giants to sign Irvin.

In 1951 Irvin finished third in the MVP race and helped the Giants into the World Series, hitting .312 with 24 home runs, 94 runs, and a National League–best 121 RBIs, and finishing third in triples, with 11. Although the Giants fell to the Yankees in that Series, four games to two, Irvin led all batters, hitting .458, going 11-for-24, with three runs scored, two RBIs, two walks, one strikeout, and two stolen bases.

Monte teamed up with Hank Thompson and Willie Mays that season to form Major League Baseball's first all-black outfield.

Irvin broke his ankle in an exhibition game in April 1952, limiting him to just 46 games that season, when he hit .310, with four home runs and 21 RBIs. Although he was named a National League All-Star that year, his only All-Star selection, he did not appear in the game.

He returned to the World Series in 1954, as the Giants defeated the Indians in four games. In two Series, Irvin hit a combined .394.

In 764 games over his eight-season major-league career, Irvin hit .293 with 99 home runs, 443 RBIs, and 366 runs scored.

With all he accomplished, it's the first game of his first World Series he remembers most.

The first game of the World Series in 1951, when I was on third base with two outs, I stole home safely, and that was one of the highlights of my career. When I think about it now, I still get a thrill from it. It was the first time it'd ever been done in 30 years. I had stolen home that year five times. The secret in stealing home is to get a good lead, make sure you take, like, an extra foot so

New York Giants left fielder Monte Irvin slides home in the first inning of the World Series opener at Yankee Stadium on October 4, 1951, as he makes the first home-plate steal in a World Series game in 30 years.

that you can slide in there safely. And I did. And when the umpire called me safe, I remember Yogi saying, "No, no!" I said, "Yeah, yeah, Yogi!" He said, "How do you know?" I said, "Tomorrow you'll see it on the front page of the *Daily News* and the *Daily Mirror.*" And sure enough, it was there. Got in by about six inches. The pitcher was Allie Reynolds, the umpire was [Bill] Summers, and of course, the catcher was Yogi Berra [Right-handed hitter Bobby Thomson was at bat]. It was the first inning, 1951, Giants versus the Yankees, and it put us up 1–0. We won that game 5–1. Every run counted.

I wasn't on my own stealing home. I had to ask [Giants manager Leo] Durocher. I asked him if I could go, and he said, "Yeah, go ahead. Get a big lead and go ahead on the next pitch." And that's what I did. I had done it before, so he knew I had success at it. I had the technique of sliding in safely, you know. I had never been caught stealing home. I think every time I tried it, I made it. So I had some pretty good successes. You see, they didn't figure on it. Of course, like I said, the secret is to get a big lead. And they didn't know I could run as fast as I did. For a big man, I could do the 100-yard dash in 10 seconds, and that was pretty good back in those days.

Oh, yeah. I have a pretty good memory, and I can remember almost everything that happened in my career, particularly the outstanding things. So that is very vivid in my mind, even still today.

Whitey Ford

Edward Charles Ford
Born: October 21, 1928, in New York, New York
MLB debut: July 1, 1950
Final game: May 21, 1967
Team: New York Yankees (1950, 1953–1967)
Primary position: Pitcher
Bats: Left—**Throws:** Left
Hall of Fame induction: 1974
Vote: 284 votes of 365 ballots cast, 77.81%

A native New Yorker, Whitey Ford spent his entire 16-year career with the Yankees. While his blond hair may have been the reason for the nickname "Whitey," it was his big-game proficiency that earned him the honor of being called "Chairman of the Board," while his mound cunning led to another moniker: "Slick."

Ford won his first nine decisions, finishing his rookie year of 1950 9–1 in 20 games, 12 starts, with one save and a 2.81 ERA. He was named the Sporting News Rookie of the Year, finishing second to Boston's Walt Dropo in BBWAA balloting. An eight-time All-Star, he started three Midsummer Classics.

Whitey served in the army during the Korean War, in 1951 and '52, returned to the Yankees for the 1953 season.

Although the coveted no-hitter escaped him, in 1955 the left-hander pitched back-to-back one-hitters in starts against Washington and Kansas City (with one hitless inning in relief against Washington sandwiched in between). Ford led the

American League in many categories throughout his career, including complete games and wins in 1955; ERA and winning percentage in 1956; ERA and shutouts in 1958; shutouts in 1960; and games started, innings pitched, wins, and winning percentage in both 1961 and 1963. He earned the Cy Young Award in 1961, going 25–4 in 39 starts, with a 3.21 ERA.

In 498 games (438 starts) over his career, Whitey compiled a record of 236–106, a .690 winning percentage, best among all pitchers with at least 300 career decisions, and best among left-handed pitchers in the 20th century with 100 or more wins.

In 11 World Series, with the Yankees winning six titles, Ford has a combined record of 10–8—more World Series wins than any other pitcher—with a 2.71 ERA. In 146 World Series innings, he allowed 44 earned runs, 132 hits, and 34 walks. His 94 career World Series strikeouts are still a record. In 1960, although the Yankees lost to the Pirates, Ford threw two complete-game shutout victories in Games 3 and 6. He followed that performance the following year, leading the Yankees over the Reds with a complete-game shutout in Game 1, and throwing five innings of a shutout in Game 4. He was named the Series MVP. He pitched a then-record 33 scoreless World Series innings.

Whitey has more World Series Game 1 starts—eight—than any other pitcher and more World Series innings, 146.

It's no surprise, then, that it's difficult for him to find just one favorite game.

I think when we won the five straight World Series games, that was special. There were a lot of great moments. But a favorite game? Not really. I pitched in a lot of World Series games, but I couldn't pick one out and say it was my favorite. I think there were too many of them.

I just go back to winning the five World Series games in a row [two in 1960, two in 1961, one in 1962]. It's not something I did, it's something the team did, but we had a lot of great moments. It was fantastic to win five in a row. There's nothing like that. There were good teams in the league too then—Detroit, the White Sox. It was great.

We didn't know we were going to win five in a row, so each one was special. And not that the World Series shares were very much like they are now. But I think it was eight or nine thousand dollars for the winning share. But when you're making $10,000 a year, that's a nice bonus to get at the end of the year.

Ralph Kiner

Ralph McPherran Kiner
Born: October 27, 1922, in Santa Rita, New Mexico
MLB debut: April 16, 1946
Final game: September 25, 1955
Teams: Pittsburgh Pirates (1946–1953), Chicago Cubs
    (1953–1954), Cleveland Indians (1955)
Primary position: Left field
Bats: Right—**Throws:** Right
Hall of Fame induction: 1975
Vote: 273 votes of 362 ballots cast, 75.41%

Although his career was cut short by injuries, Ralph Kiner's prodigious offensive output put him among the leaders in the National League for most of his 10 seasons. The six-time All-Star for the Pittsburgh Pirates led the league in home runs for each of his first seven seasons, more than doubling his rookie output of 23 in 1946 to 51 in his sophomore season. His 54 roundtrippers in 1949 were 18 more than Stan Musial, who was second with 36, and 11 ahead of Ted Williams, who led the American League with 43.

Kiner became the first National League player with two 50-plus home-run seasons, in 1947 and 1949. He led the majors a record six consecutive times in home runs, from 1947 through 1952—tying Johnny Mize in 1947 with 51 and in 1948 with 40, and matching Hank Sauer with 37 in 1952.

Kiner led the league in slugging percentage in 1947 (.639), 1949 (.658), and 1951 (.627) and in on-base-plus-slugging percentage in 1947 (1.055), 1949 (1.089), and 1951 (1.079). He holds the major-league record of eight home runs in four straight multiple-home-run games, a feat he accomplished in September 1947.

His most productive season was arguably 1949, when he finished fourth in the NL MVP voting, behind Jackie Robinson, Musial, and Enos Slaughter. That season he led the league in slugging percentage (.658), home runs (54), RBIs (127), walks (117), and at-bats per home runs (10.2). He was also among the leaders in batting average (.310, fifth), on-base percentage (.432, third), games played (152, ninth), runs scored (116, fourth), total bases (361, second), extra-base hits (78, second), and times on base (288, fourth).

Kiner was traded to the Chicago Cubs as part of a 10-player deal in June 1953. After the 1954 season, he was the player to be named later, completing an earlier deal between the Cubs and the Cleveland Indians. Two days shy of his 33rd birthday, he was released by the Indians after the 1955 season.

Slowed by back injuries, Kiner elected to retire, finishing his career with a .279 average, 1,015 RBIs, and 369 home runs. With 5,205 at-bats, Kiner homered an average of every 14.10 at-bats. He also hit five home runs in two consecutive games twice. In 1999 he was ranked 90th on *The Sporting News* list of 100 Greatest Baseball Players.

His playing days over, Kiner began broadcasting, completing his 47th season calling games for the New York Mets in 2008.

Warren Spahn once said of the slugger, "Ralph Kiner can wipe out your lead with one swing." Which Kiner proved in one memorable All-Star Game.

———————————

We were playing in the All-Star Game in 1950, and I was with the National League, of course. My first time up I hit a ball to left field that Ted Williams caught against the fence, and broke his elbow. But at the time no one realized that he had broken it, and he played eight more innings. So that in itself was amazing. But it was a memorable game for me, because I hit a home run in the ninth inning to tie the game up. And it was off Art Houtteman. The game then went on to 14 innings and then the National League won when Red Schoendienst hit a home run off of Ted Gray. And he won the game. That was really one of the great games that I was involved in at that time. So that would be one of my big memories.

That certainly is very clear in my memory because the National League at that time hadn't won against the American League in quite a while [since 1944], and that sort of turned the tables on the National League winning that game. In fact, before the game started Warren Giles, who [became] president of the National League [the next season], came into our clubhouse and made a speech like, "C'mon, you guys, we want to win this game. So let's play." And most of the starting lineup played the whole game. They didn't really put in any substitutes. So we had Schoendienst as a pinch hitter, if you can believe that, who hit the home run and won it. I tied it up with a home run off Houtteman to make it go into extra innings.

I remember that game very well. It was a very hot day in Chicago. We played in old Comiskey Park. It was a hot game. In those days, we didn't fly. We took trains everywhere, to all the cities. So it was a matter of getting the game over with so we could catch our trains to go back and restart the season.

All-Star Games certainly meant something then. And it was no secret that the National League was embarrassed that they hadn't won in quite some time. At that time it was very important. I think they were taken more seriously then. The overall thinking, aside from the fact that they made a big thing out of having the winning team be the home team in the World Series, which I certainly think is ridiculous, certainly should not be put into that perspective, because it's still an exhibition game and it shouldn't have an effect on what happens in the World Series later on in the year. But it was done for television and to hype that game.

But that was really a great game. I think the fact that the players stayed in the entire game was very important. And it wasn't really the old theory of an exhibition game and showing off the stars of baseball. It was more a thing where the National League wanted to win and the American League wanted to continue to win.

I think there was more pride involved back then. But the game has changed so much. Nowadays, with free agency, you have players who move around much more, which in those days, back in the 1950s, players usually stayed with a team on a fairly permanent basis. So there was more rivalry and less camaraderie than you might have now in baseball, because the players play in different leagues and different teams quite often now. It's a different game.

I was in a few All-Star Games. I hit home runs in three consecutive All-Star Games. And that was one of them right there. It really was important to the National League. I'm the only one that's ever done that, hit home runs in three straight. So far! But I think that would be the one game I remember. We had a full house. It was a big game. And then, of course, Chicago was a great baseball city. And the other thing that was interesting was that Williams stayed in that game and played into the ninth inning, when he finally left. One of his regrets later on was that he said that he could never really hit again after he'd broken his elbow, but that wasn't really true because he hit, like, .380 after that [.388 in 1957 at the age of 38]. He could hit. But that was a big part of that game.

I'm really happy I was able to be a part of it.

Robin Roberts

Robin Evan Roberts
Born: September 30, 1926, in Springfield, Illinois
MLB debut: June 18, 1948
Final game: September 3, 1966
Teams: Philadelphia Phillies (1948–1961), Baltimore Orioles
(1962–1965), Houston Astros (1965–1966), Chicago Cubs
(1966)
Primary position: Pitcher
Bats: Switch—**Throws:** Right
Hall of Fame induction: 1976
Vote: 337 votes of 388 ballots cast, 86.86%

Although he started off as a basketball player at Michigan State University, Robin Roberts would leave his mark in baseball.

Roberts was 21 when he made his major-league debut shortly after signing with the Phillies in 1948 on his way to a 19-season career, compiling a record of 286–245 with a 3.40 ERA, 45 shutouts, 2,357 strikeouts, 902 walks, and 4,582 hits over 4,689 innings in his career.

In 1950 he began a string of six consecutive 20-win seasons, but his streak was broken in 1956 when he had 19 wins. His 28 wins in 1952 were the most in the National League since Dizzy Dean's 30 in 1934, and only Denny McLain, with 31 in 1968, has passed that mark since.

Of his 609 career starts, Roberts recorded 305 complete games. He pitched more than 250 innings in 10 seasons, including six straight seasons with more than 300 innings, never walking more than 77 batters in a season.

A seven-time All-Star, Roberts was named the Major League Player of the Year and The Sporting News Pitcher of the Year in 1952 when he established a record of 28–7, with 30 complete games in his 37 starts, and a 2.59 ERA in 330 innings. He was also named The Sporting News Pitcher of the Year in 1955 with a record of 23–14, with a 3.28 ERA and 26 complete games in 38 starts. He finished in the top 10 in MVP voting five times, including 1952, when he was ranked second. In 1999 Roberts was ranked 74th on *The Sporting News* list of 100 Greatest Baseball Players.

On May 13, 1954, he allowed a leadoff home run to Cincinnati's Bobby Adams, then set down the next 27 batters on his way to an 8–1 win, and one of his three one-hitters. He is also the only pitcher in history to record wins against the Boston Braves, Milwaukee Braves, and Atlanta Braves, and holds the major-league record for most consecutive Opening Day starts for the same team, with 12 for the Phillies from 1950 to 1961.

Roberts led the league in wins in 1952 (28), 1953 (23), 1954 (23), and 1955 (23); walks-and-hits-per-innings-pitched ratio in 1954 (1.025); walks per nine innings in 1952 (1.23), 1953 (1.58), 1954 (1.50), and 1956 (1.21); innings pitched in 1951 (315); 1952 (330), 1953 (346⅔), 1954 (336⅔), and 1955 (305); strikeouts in 1953 (198) and 1954 (185); starts in 1950 (39), 1951 (39), 1952 (37), 1953 (41), 1954 (38), and 1955 (38); complete games in 1952 (30), 1953 (33), 1954 (29), 1955 (26), and 1956 (22); shutouts in 1950 (5); and strikeouts-to-walks ratio in 1952 (3.29), 1953 (3.25), 1954 (3.30), 1956 (3.93), and 1959 (3.91).

In 1950 Roberts led the Phillies' "Whiz Kids" to their first pennant in 35 seasons, starting three of their final five games, including the last game of the season, besting the Dodgers for his 20th win of the season, his first 20-win campaign, and the Phillies' first 20-game winner since Grover Cleveland Alexander in 1917.

The final game in 1950, we played on Ebbets Field. We had to beat the Dodgers to win the pennant. If we'd lost that day, we'd have been tied and had to have a playoff. [But] we won 4–1 in 10 innings. I pitched for the Phillies, and Don Newcombe pitched for the Dodgers. Dick Sisler hit a three-run home run in the top of the tenth, and Richie Ashburn threw out Cal Abrams in the bottom of the ninth, or else we wouldn't have had a tenth inning. But it was great.

I joined the Phillies in 1948, and we came in way down [sixth], in '49 we came in third, and then in '50 we won the pennant, which was the first pennant the Phillies had won since 1915. So it was 35 years, and it was exciting for the city and for us. For me, when I think of my career, that's the one game that stands out more than any other, because of all that it meant. We had had a seven-and-a-half-game lead with about 10 or 12 to go, and we'd blown that. And we had a one-game lead with one to go, and we were able to win it. And to be the first time, we naturally felt we were going to do more of them, but that was the only one I was ever involved in.

There were a number there that were tough hitters. Snider was there and Jackie Robinson. The Dodgers were an outstanding club. We had had trouble with them before. We had played against them pretty well in 1950, and, of course, winning that game at the end was really icing on the cake for us. But they were an outstanding baseball team. They won in '49, and in the playoffs in '51 they lost. They won again in '52. They were one of the outstanding clubs. We did have a year where we played them pretty even, and that's why we won the pennant.

Newcombe and I had pitched against each other quite often. I was fortunate against him on a number of occasions. But it was always 4–1, 3–2, 2–1, that type of thing. And both of us would pitch the whole ballgame. We had quite a history there for two or three years, and I remember that game particularly because Newcombe pitched so well for them. But of course he may remember it for a different reason. He was a beautiful pitcher and also an excellent hitter. Don was quite an athlete.

At the end of that season Bubba Church got hit in the eye with a line drive, so he was out for the rest of the season. That happened about the middle of September. Curt [Simmons] was called up into the National Guard on September 10; we were seven games in front when he left. He was just as good a pitcher as there was in baseball at the time. That really hurt us. We would have won much earlier if he'd still been with us. And Bob Miller, another starter, had hurt his back. So we ended up a little short, as far as the pitchers go. So they got me involved. I started three games in the last five days. I wouldn't recommend it, but it turned out all right.

After that last game I was excited and exhausted. It was just something, you know, you look back on, and when you're 23 you can do things like that and it doesn't bother you that much physically. That was also my first time winning 20 games, and after that I was able to win six years in a row. The seventh year I won 19, but it's interesting how that extra game is something people notice. No one's ever said I almost won seven, they say I won six.

But, yes, that game just jumps out. There's nothing else that's close. I enjoyed so many of them, but when you ask me for one that was more important than any of the others, it was that one. It was the day after my 24th birthday.

At that time you didn't give thought to the complete games. Other guys did it, too. Spahnie did it, and Larry Jansen, and Johnny Antonelli. It was just common practice that, if a guy was doing all right, you leave him in. And we didn't think anything of it. I didn't give it one thought, to be honest with you. When I went out there, I thought I was supposed to pitch the whole game, and in most cases I got to. It was a nice habit. It's different now. They have trainers and they have more pitchers than they use, and it's an accepted practice that is a completely different approach to it. And, of course, I won't get the opportunity to try it but it might not be a bad idea. I don't know how many pitches I'd throw in a game. I never even counted them. But I would imagine between 100 and 125 would probably be a normal game, sometimes less, sometimes more, but most of the time in that area.

That was my only postseason, 1950. I remember my wife said she wasn't much of a ball fan. Back then she said she thought we would be in the playoffs every fall. I misled her.

But the memories come right back. Oh, no doubt. I could tell you the pitch count and everything about it. It was a phenomenal memory for me and it still is. That was such an important game.

Ernie Banks

Ernest Banks
Born: January 31, 1931, in Dallas, Texas
MLB debut: September 17, 1953
Final game: September 26, 1971
Teams: Chicago Cubs (1953–1971)
Primary position: Shortstop
Bats: Right—**Throws:** Right
Hall of Fame induction: 1977
Vote: 321 votes of 383 ballots cast, 83.81%

"Let's play two!" Ernie Banks, "Mr. Cub," is beloved by Cubs fans not only for his love of the game and sunny disposition but also for the excellent all-around career he established in 19 seasons.

After playing with the Kansas City Monarchs of the Negro Leagues, Banks signed as an amateur free agent with the Cubs in 1953, becoming the team's first African American player, appearing in 10 games that season. In 1954 he finished second (to the Cardinals' Wally Moon) in the National League Rookie of the Year voting, hitting .275 with 19 home runs and 79 RBIs. In 19 seasons, Ernie hit .274 with a .500 slugging percentage, 2,583 hits, 512 home runs, and 1,636 RBIs.

In 1958 and 1959 he became the first NL player to win back-to-back MVP awards. In 1958 he hit .313 with a .614 slugging percentage, 193 hits, 47 home runs, and 129 RBIs. He followed that by hitting .304, with a .596 slugging percentage, 179 hits, 45 home runs, and 143 RBIs in 1959.

In 1955 he hit 44 home runs, breaking Vern Stephens' record for roundtrippers by a shortstop. From 1955 through 1960, Banks hit more home runs, 248, than any other player.

Although not known for defense early in his career, in 1959 he set since-broken records for fewest errors by a shortstop in a season, with 12, and best fielding percentage at .985.

In 1999 he was named to baseball's All-Century Team and was ranked 38th on *The Sporting News* list of 100 Greatest Baseball Players.

Ernie led the league in slugging percentage in 1958 (.614); games played in 1954 (154), 1955 (154), 1957 (156), 1958 (154), 1959 (155), and 1960 (156); at-bats in 1958 (617); total bases in 1958 (379); home runs in 1958 (47) and 1960 (41); RBIs in 1958 (129) and 1959 (143); extra-base hits in 1955 (82), 1957 (83), 1958 (81), and 1960 (80); intentional walks in 1959 (20) and 1960 (28); and at-bats per home runs in 1958 (13.1).

From 1962 until the end of his playing career in 1971, Banks played first base and ultimately played more games there (1,259), than at his Hall of Fame position, shortstop (1,125).

Although he played in 2,528 games without making it to the postseason, Banks played in 13 All-Star Games, including two each in 1959, 1960, and 1962. He started six All-Star Games at short and one at first base. There is one particular Midsummer Classic that stands out, not so much for what he did but for what it meant to him.

———————

O h my, oh my, oh my. Everything has been so wonderful in my life. I cannot single out one game. I've had no-hitters. Kenny Holtzman pitched a no-hitter against the Braves. There are so many wonderful games, so many. Let's see. I played an All-Star Game in Boston one year. I faced Camilo Pascual, and he struck me out. That's one game I remember. That was my first time at Fenway. That was [July 31] 1961. He had four strikeouts, and I was one of them.

That was my first time in Fenway. It was really exciting to see the Wall and be in the same park that so many great players had played in: Ted Williams, Jackie Jensen. Jackie won the MVP Award the same year I did, and we became friends through that. That was a memorable game for me, but it was not because of the game—because it was a tie game. So we didn't win. Nobody won. No harm, no foul.

But that was the game for me. My first time in Boston. My first time in Fenway. And then I had a friend who played for the Red Sox, Pumpsie Green. He was the first African American who played for the Red Sox, and that was important for me. Being in Boston, being in Fenway, that was so important to me at that time. I thought about it before I got to Boston, and I was excited about getting there. And coming into Logan International. It was very nice to be there in such a new airport in a famous place. And then you go through a tunnel under the river. And my love has always been education, and being in Boston with all these great universities—Harvard, Radcliffe, MIT, Boston College. I wasn't able to see a lot of that but just being in a city where there is so much education and talent and people who've done so many things around the world. Henry Kissinger went to Harvard. It was just an exciting place, and I could feel it when I was there. Then the park itself, the city itself, it was just a wonderful place to be. I wish I could have stayed longer. It was just too short, and it was a 1–1 tie game.

And Camilo Pascual got me. I had not faced him before, but I had heard a lot about him, what a great pitcher he was. And he proved that against the All-Stars. So it was just a very memorable time. I enjoyed it. It was fun, and I'll always remember it. It was just so exciting. I really enjoyed it. It was a great memory for me, and that was the only time I played at Fenway.

I was there again in 1999 at the All-Star Game. Ted Williams was there and all the players. Those were two special days in my life.

Al Kaline

Albert William Kaline
Born: December 19, 1934, in Baltimore, Maryland
MLB debut: June 25, 1953
Final game: October 2, 1974
Team: Detroit Tigers (1953–1974)
Primary position: Right field
Bats: Right—**Throws:** Right
Hall of Fame induction: 1980
Vote: 340 votes of 385 ballots cast, 88.31%

Al Kaline signed with the Detroit Tigers just after midnight on the evening of his graduation from Southern High School in Baltimore. Exactly a week after his high school graduation he made his major-league debut, never having played a game in the minors.

In 1955, his second full season in the big leagues, Kaline won the American League batting title with a .340 mark. At just 20 years old, Kaline was the youngest player to win a batting championship in history, drawing inevitable comparisons to Tigers great Ty Cobb, who was a day older than Kaline when he won the title in 1907. Kaline, Alan Trammell, and Cobb are the only Tigers to play 20 or more seasons in a Detroit uniform.

While that was Kaline's only batting title—he finished second in 1959, 1961, and 1963—over 22 seasons he compiled a .297 average with 3,007 hits, 399 home runs, and 1,583 RBIs. He was runner-up in the American League MVP

Al Kaline leaps to catch Mickey Mantle's try for a home run in the first inning of a game at Tiger Stadium in Detroit on September 16, 1961.

voting in 1955 (to Yankees catcher Yogi Berra), and again in 1963 (to Yankees catcher Elston Howard). However, *The Sporting News* named Kaline its Player of the Year in both those seasons.

Consistently among the league leaders at the plate throughout his career, Kaline hit over .300 in nine seasons, including 1972, when he hit .313, his highest average since 1961, when he was 37. He also hit 20 or more home runs in nine seasons. On April 17, 1955, he had three home runs—off three different pitchers—against the Kansas City Athletics, including two in the sixth inning. He reached the vaunted 3,000-hits milestone in his hometown of Baltimore on September 24, 1974, hitting a double off the Orioles' Dave McNally.

Known as much for his defensive prowess as for his offensive skills, Kaline earned 10 Gold Gloves in his career and was selected for 15 All-Star teams. With his strong arm, Kaline primarily played right field, where he had 116 assists in 1,745 games, and once threw out two base runners at home in the same inning. He had a streak of 242 consecutive errorless games, committing just 82 miscues in 2,625 career games, for a .987 career fielding percentage.

He led the Tigers to the 1968 World Series—Detroit's first in 23 seasons—hitting .379 with two home runs and eight RBIs and was the 10th player elected to the Hall of Fame in his first year of eligibility. In 1999 Kaline was ranked No. 76 on *The Sporting News* list of 100 Greatest Baseball Players.

An all-around ballplayer and model of consistency, Brooks Robinson once said of Kaline, "There have been a lot of great defensive players. The fella who could do everything is Al Kaline. He was just the epitome of what a great outfielder is all about—great speed, catches the ball, and throws the ball well."

A great all-around player, Kaline remembers an offensive game and a game in which his glove was the star.

Oh, a favorite game is really hard to pick. But personally, I hit three home runs in one game in 1955. I hit two home runs in one inning. It was a game that certainly I remember, and it's still part of Detroit history, since there's only been one other player to do it. [On April 17, 1955, against the Kansas City A's at Briggs Stadium, Kaline went 4-for-5, with three runs scored, six RBIs, a walk, a three-run home run in the third inning, and a solo shot and a two-run homer in the sixth, as the Tigers won 16–0.]

But the game I really think would be my favorite is a game against the Yankees. Bottom of the ninth inning, Mantle at the plate. Tigers are leading by one run, and Mantle hits the ball in old Yankee Stadium where the bullpen was fairly low. Mel Allen was the announcer. And I jumped with one foot up on the fence. I made the catch, but Mel Allen called, "Mantle hits the home run to win the ballgame!" Of course, the clubhouse guy in the visiting clubhouse turns off the radio because he knows the Tigers are going to be very upset. So, from what I understand, the Tigers come running in, and they're all happy and smiling, and he says, "What happened? You lost." And someone said, "No, Kaline made the catch." So that game stands out, first of all because of Mantle, who I thought was one of the best, and Mel Allen, the great announcer who was making the call. So that really stands out in my mind.

Oh, yeah, I was always a better defensive player than an offensive player. I could always help the team defensively. I mean, you can't get a hit every time you want to. But there's no reason in the world why you can't help the team defensively.

Any time we played the Yankees we knew we had to be on. I used to love playing against the Yankees, but I knew playing in right field I was always going to get a lot of action out there because of the guys that they had on the team. Skowron hit the ball to right field all the time.

Elston Howard hit the ball the other way all the time. And, of course, they had Maris, and Mantle, and guys like Yogi, naturally. So I always knew I had to be ready. And I really looked forward to playing the Yankees all the time. It was great because of the atmosphere. The fans were always there, and it was real challenge.

Coming off the field after making a play off Mickey Mantle, my favorite player in the American League, and winning the game in Yankee Stadium was a great feeling. And also knowing I did something to help the team win. But any time you do something great in New York it's exposed a lot more than any place else. So it's a great feeling.

I just remember the look on the clubhouse guy's face when I came in, saying, "I thought you guys lost, and everybody comes in and they're all happy!"

Hank Aaron

Henry Louis Aaron
Born: February 5, 1934, in Mobile, Alabama
MLB debut: April 13, 1954
Final game: October 3, 1976
Teams: Milwaukee Braves (1954–1965), Atlanta Braves
    (1966–1974), Milwaukee Brewers (1975–1976)
Primary position: Right field
Bats: Right—**Throws:** Right
Hall of Fame induction: 1982
Vote: 406 votes of 415 ballots cast, 97.83%

It is fitting that Hank Aaron is the first player in the alphabetical roster of Hall of Famers—and likely always will be. Aaron began his career as a high school junior with the semipro Mobile Black Bears, and then the Indianapolis Clowns of the Negro Leagues before signing as an 18-year-old free agent with the Boston Braves on June 14, 1952. Aaron was the last of the Negro Leaguers to play in the major leagues.

For more than 33 years "Hammerin' Hank" was baseball's all-time home-run king, with 755 career roundtrippers. Although he never reached 50 home runs in a season—the most he hit was 47 in 1971—Aaron had 20 consecutive seasons of 20 or more homers, and is the only player to have 15 seasons of 30 or more home runs. He had 150 or more hits in 17 consecutive seasons, and at least 100 RBIs in 11 seasons, including five straight from 1959 through 1963.

Hank Aaron eyes the flight of the ball after hitting his 715th career home run in a game against the Los Angeles Dodgers in Atlanta on April 8, 1974.

Hank holds the all-time record for total bases, with 6,856; extra-base hits, with 1,477; and RBIs, with 2,297; and is second with 12,364 at-bats; third with 3,771 hits and 3,298 games; and tied with Babe Ruth for fourth, with 2,174 runs scored.

In 1957 he was named the National League MVP, hitting .322, with 44 home runs and 132 RBIs. On September 23, he hit an eleventh-inning home run off St. Louis's Billy Muffett, clinching the 1957 National League pennant for the Braves—their first in Milwaukee. Leading the Braves to the World Series, Aaron hit .393 with three home runs and seven RBIs against the Yankees.

He also finished in the top five in MVP voting in seven other seasons. His play in right field earned him the Gold Glove in three consecutive seasons, from 1958 through 1960.

Aaron appeared in more All-Star Games than any other player. Named to 21 rosters in his 23-year career, Aaron went to 24 games for the National League and one for the American League, including 1959, 1960, 1961, and 1962, when two Midsummer Classics were played each season (although he did not play in the first of two 1962 games).

Despite his impressive stats and accomplishments, Aaron is perhaps best remembered for the grace and humility he exhibited throughout his career, and especially in his quest to break Babe Ruth's all-time home-run record when he was subjected to death threats and racial slurs.

On Aaron's 65th birthday, February 5, 1999, Major League Baseball announced the creation of the Hank Aaron Award, honoring the best offensive players in the National League and American League. It was the first major award initiated in more than 30 years and the only award named after a living former player. Later that year he was named to baseball's All-Century Team and was ranked No. 5 on *The Sporting News* list of 100 Greatest Baseball Players.

In June 2002 Aaron was awarded the Presidential Medal of Freedom, the nation's highest civilian honor. The White House press release read, "Hank Aaron is one of the most accomplished players in the history of baseball. Aaron holds the career records for home runs (755 in his 23-year career), runs batted in, and total bases. He was inducted into the Baseball Hall of Fame in 1982. Mr. Aaron played first on a professional Negro League team, and was then recruited by the Milwaukee Braves and sent to a minor league team in Jacksonville, Florida, where he was one of the first black players to break the color line in the deep South. Mr. Aaron was undeterred in his pursuit of excellence by frequent encounters with racism throughout his career."

With all his historic accomplishments, it is difficult to pick just one game. But Hank has a fondness for his first Midsummer Classic.

Y ou know, I think my favorite is the first All-Star Game in Milwaukee [July 12, 1955]. We were behind at the time. I don't believe Willie Mays started, myself, Stan Musial. We all went in as subs later in the game. And I remember that game, and this is the truth: I remember Stan Musial walking up and down the dugout, and he said, "You know what? They don't pay us to play overtime." And he went up and hit a home run. He hit a home run, and we won the game. And that is the truth. We beat the American League in Milwaukee, and that was my first All-Star Game.

Because it was my first All-Star Game and Stan Musial, who happened to be one of my idols, hit a home run, that was one of the greatest moments I ever had. Three things happened: I played in the game, Stan Musial hit a home run [his only hit of the game], and the National League won [6–5 in 12 innings].

Other than All-Star Games? I can't pick out one. I wish I could. I got a few to choose from, but I don't know if I can pick out just one. I've just got too many. But that one was special.

George Kell

George Clyde Kell
Born: August 23, 1922, in Swifton, Arkansas
MLB debut: September 28, 1943
Final game: September 14, 1957
Teams: Philadelphia A's (1943–1946), Detroit Tigers (1946–1952), Boston Red Sox (1952–1954), Chicago White Sox (1954–1956), Baltimore Orioles (1956–1957)
Primary position: Third base
Bats: Right—**Throws:** Right
Hall of Fame induction: 1983
Vote: Elected to the Hall of Fame by the Veterans Committee

Although he was originally signed by the Brooklyn Dodgers as an amateur free agent in 1940, George Kell never appeared in a game for the Dodgers, who sent him to Lancaster of the Interstate League in 1942. The Philadelphia A's then purchased Kell, who made his big-league debut with the A's. But it was with the Detroit Tigers that Kell established himself as a future Hall of Famer.

Equally adept both at the plate and in the field, Kell was consistently among the league leaders both offensively and defensively. He hit over .300 nine times in his 15-year career, including eight consecutive seasons, and led the league in hits in 1950 (218) and in 1951 (191). Kell led the league in doubles in 1950 (56), and with 36 in 1951, when he was also the league leader in singles (150). In 1946 and 1956 he topped the AL in sacrifice hits, with 15 and 14, respectively.

Kell was known for his sure hands and strong, accurate arm. Considered the finest third baseman in the American League in the late 1940s and early 1950s, Kell led AL third basemen in fielding percentage seven times and led the league in double plays six times, assists four times, and putouts twice.

A 10-time All-Star, including eight straight selections from 1947 through 1954, Kell received more All-Star votes than any other player in either league in 1950 and played all 14 innings of that Midsummer Classic, with two RBIs in the AL's 4–3 loss.

In 1949 Kell narrowly—and dramatically—captured the AL title, edging out Ted Williams by less than two ten-thousandths of a point, .34291 to .34276, on the season's final day, stopping Williams's bid to become the first player to capture three Triple Crowns. It was Kell's only batting title. He finished second—to Williams's teammate Billy Goodman—the next season, while leading the league in hits with 218. Kell holds the record for fewest strikeouts by a batting champion, with just 13 whiffs in 1949.

In his 15-year career, he played in 1,795 games, hitting .306 with 2,054 hits, 385 doubles, 50 triples, 78 home runs, 870 RBIs, 881 runs scored, 51 stolen bases, 621 walks, a .414 slugging percentage, a .367 on-base percentage, and 287 strikeouts.

In 1,692 games at third base, he had a .969 fielding percentage, with 1,825 putouts, 3,303 assists, 306 double plays, and just 166 errors.

After debuting as a 21-year-old with the A's, Kell retired 14 seasons later from the Baltimore Orioles and began broadcasting games, first with the Orioles, then with CBS television and NBC radio. With the exception of 1964, Kell called Tigers games from 1959 to 1996, retiring from broadcasting prior to the 1997 season.

With 6,702 at-bats in 1,795 games, one at-bat stands out for him.

I have so many fond memories of those 14 years. But I do remember my first time at bat in the major leagues. I hit a three-base hit. I thought this was going to be an easy, easy thing. I had just come up from a Class B team, where I'd done well that year. And I hit a triple the first time up, and I said, "Well, this isn't hard at all." Then I didn't get another hit for a few days!

The pitcher was a left-hander from [the St. Louis Browns], Al Milnar. He was a veteran pitcher. I talked to him a couple of years ago and I was asking him if he remembered seeing me my first time at bat, and he said, "I sure do." I doubt he did. But I remember him well because I was just a 21-year-old kid.

Well, I was probably scared to death. I came up from Lancaster at a Class B league, where I'd led all the minor leagues in hitting. I hit .396, and I probably was full of myself. But I was a good hitter. And I walked out on the diamond and I was probably scared to death. I had a triple my first time up and then I didn't get another hit. But that was a good way to start off.

We were in Philadelphia, at Shibe Park. Mr. Connie Mack had bought my contract.

Dick Siebert played first base, he was a veteran. And Hal Wagner was the catcher, a veteran ballplayer. And the infield was all minor leaguers that Mr. Mack had brought up at the end of the season. And in the outfield later he

George Kell bats in a spring-training game against the Cincinnati Reds on March 11, 1943, in Lakeland, Florida.

had [Sam] Chapman, a fine ballplayer. We had [Bobby] Estalella, a Cuban ballplayer.

I didn't really get any advice from the veterans. Mr. Mack was about 80 years old and didn't want anybody fooling with his kids and giving them advice. He'd do all of that. One coach was his assistant manager—he was a lot younger and had played for Mr. Mack for many years—and he did most of the talking: you'll do this and you'll do that, you're going to hit here and you're going to hit there. And we listened to him. Mr. Mack did not comment a whole lot to his ballplayers except to say very nice things. He was a very soft-spoken man.

I was just about 21 years old, but it really does seem like it was just yesterday. I can't help but tell everybody that I've been the luckiest man on the face of the earth. I went to the major leagues when I was 20 years old. I should have been farmed out probably and sent to the minors for another year or two or three. But Mr. Mack kept me on the team, and I gradually got better. And then he sold me to Detroit two years later, traded me to Detroit for Barney McCosky. And things just went great in Detroit. I hit .300 for the next nine years—well, for the seven years I was there but nine in all.

And I've just been the luckiest man on the face of the earth. The thing I most wanted to do—be a big-league ballplayer—has come true. And then after I got through playing ball, I retired, came home. I was going to farm. I'd bought some farmland here in Swifton [Arkansas]. I was going to farm and be with my family for the rest of my life. And all of a sudden the Tigers called and said, "Come back and broadcast." And I went back and did the television games for the next 37 years. So how lucky can you be? But I finally just had to walk away, and I hated to do it. I hated to tell [Tigers owner] Mr. Ilitch that I was worn out. I was getting old and I was getting tired, and my family was getting grumpy waiting for me to come home all the time. But I have not regretted it. I quit at the end of the 1996 season.

I went up for the final game of the playoffs in 2006 and threw out the first ball. And they won that and went into the World Series. It was a great thrill for me. But I'm living here in Arkansas, right in the center of Cardinals territory. They don't know anybody else exists! They made it pretty hard on me.

The memories of that first game come right back. Yes, they do. I just think of the time I spent in Philadelphia. Just a flat-out kid. I only played that one ballgame that year. And this is ironic. My wife and I were childhood sweethearts all through high school. And she went off to college when I went off to play ball. And after two years of college they offered her a teaching job here in Swifton, and she came back to teach school. Mr. Mack bought my contract on Monday and wanted me to be there on Tuesday. And I told him I sure would, I'd love to, I'll be there. But I said, "Mr. Mack, I've got to go home." I explained to him my wife was teaching and they wanted me to coach basketball since I didn't have a job in the off-season. And he said, "Well, that's where you belong! And you play one game here and you're on my roster and you'll be a major-league ballplayer and, whatever happens, you'll always be a major-league ballplayer." Now, wasn't that nice of him? I played one ballgame and went home. He said, "I'll see you in spring training." I thought, "Yep, where you going to send me?" Well, he never sent me anywhere. I played there, and I never played another day in the minor leagues.

Mr. Mack was legendary. He really was. And he was so nice. A few years later, when I was playing for Detroit, my brother Skeeter, who's seven years younger than I am, came along. Skeeter was a ballplayer, and the Tigers wanted him to come up and work out with them and maybe they'd sign him. Well, he was there about four or five days and they didn't sign him. Mr. Mack came to town and saw him out there, and he called me over to the dugout. He said, "That your brother?" I said, "Yes, it is." He said, "The Tigers going to sign him?" I said, "Well, he's been here a week and they haven't yet." He said, "Well, I'll sign him. I took a chance on one Kell, I'll take a chance on another." He signed him that day.

Juan Marichal

Juan Antonio (Sanchez) Marichal
Born: October 20, 1937, in Laguna Verde, Dominican Republic
MLB debut: July 19, 1960
Final game: April 16, 1975
Teams: San Francisco Giants (1960–1973), Boston Red Sox
    (1974), Los Angeles Dodgers (1975)
Primary position: Pitcher
Bats: Right—**Throws:** Right
Hall of Fame induction: 1983
Vote: 313 votes of 374 ballots cast, 83.69%

Juan Marichal—the Dominican Dandy known for his trademark high leg kick, overpowering stuff, and intimidating presence on the mound—was the first player from the Dominican Republic inducted into the Hall of Fame. As a 22-year-old in his major-league debut, Marichal set the tone for his career—a complete-game, one-hit, 12-strikeout, one-walk shutout win over the Phillies. The lone hit he allowed in that game was a single to pinch-hitter Clay Dalrymple with two outs in the eighth inning. He finished his rookie season with a record of 6–2 and a 2.67 ERA.

In his 16-year career, 14 of which were with the San Francisco Giants, the right-hander was the winningest pitcher in the 1960s, posting more than 20 wins in six seasons and leading the National League in wins in 1963, with a record of 25–8, and in 1968, at 26–9. He also led the league in shutouts in 1965 (10) and 1969 (8); ERA in 1969 (2.10); innings pitched in 1963 (321⅓) and 1968 (326); complete games in 1964 (22) and 1968 (30); strikeouts-to-walks ratio in 1966 (6.17), 1967 (3.95), and 1968 (4.74); walks-and-hits-per-innings-pitched ratio in 1966 (.859) and 1969 (.994); and walks-per-nine-innings ratio in 1965 (1.40), 1966 (1.05), 1969 (1.62), and 1973 (1.61).

Manito compiled a career record of 243–142, a .631 winning percentage, with a 2.89 ERA and 244 complete games. With his exceptional control, Marichal issued just 709 walks, compared to 2,303 strikeouts in 3,506 career innings—a career strikeouts-to-walks ratio of 3.25. In the 1960s he posted 191 wins, more than any other National League pitcher.

A nine-time All-Star, including 1962 when two games were played, Marichal appeared in eight games and was named MVP of the 1965 Midsummer Classic, starting and throwing three scoreless innings, giving up just one hit, in the senior circuit's 6–5 win. Marichal was 2–0 with a 0.50 ERA in his All-Star appearances.

In 1969, at the age of 31, Marichal went 21–11 with a league-best 2.10 ERA in 36 starts, with 27 complete games and eight shutouts. Severe back pain nearly ended his career in 1970, when he went 12–10 with a 4.11 ERA. But he rebounded the following season, finishing with a recod of 18–11 with a 2.94 ERA, and winning the division-clinching game on the last day of the season, a complete-game victory over the Padres.

In 1999 Marichal, who went on to be the minister of sports in the Dominican Republic, was ranked No. 71 on *The Sporting News* list of 100 Greatest Baseball Players.

Despite appearing in 471 career regular-season games, it is a game on July 2, 1963—less than a month after his first and only career no-hitter—that stands out most for Marichal.

In that game he battled the Milwaukee Braves and his friend, Warren Spahn, for 16 innings, holding the Braves scoreless on eight hits and four walks, with 10 strikeouts.

When you play that many years, there are some games that come out in your mind. Like my first game in the majors: I threw a one-hitter, and in 1963 I pitched a no-hitter. But there's one game that I pitched against the great Warren Spahn. We hooked up in a game and we completed the game, 16 innings, at 1–0. And you're not going to see that anymore in baseball. So that's something that I've never forgotten.

[Giants manager] Alvin Dark wanted to take me out in the ninth inning. I begged him to let me stay in the game. So he did. After 14 innings, he wanted to take me out again. And I told him, "Mr. Dark, do you see that man pitching on the mound?" He said, "Yes." I said, "Well, that man is 42 years old. I'm only [25], and nobody is going to take me out of this game."

Juan Marichal throws a 1–0 no-hitter against the Houston Colt .45s at Candlestick Park on June 15, 1963.

In that game, I threw 227 pitches. That's another thing. You're not going to see that today. After the game, I was tired. And the next day, Warren came up to me in the tunnel that leads to the clubhouse and he gave me some pointers, how to prepare for the next game. That was very nice of him. We were very close. We were good friends. He told me what to do for the next game, what type of exercise. I never put ice on my arm or my shoulders, so he told me to take a warm-water shower, and this and that. And I did, and I was always ready for the next start.

That was in 1963. We hooked up in games many times.

I don't remember who was the toughest out in that game. After you get to the ninth inning, you want to win. I don't think there were too many guys that really hit me in that game, because it was like a machine. Warren was in, one-two-three. I go in, one-two-three. It kept on like that for 16 innings.

When I went to pitch the sixteenth inning, we were the home club. Coming back to the bench, I waited for Willie Mays to come from center field around the first-base line. And I told him, "Willie, Alvin Dark's mad at me. He's not going to let me stay any longer." So he told me, "Don't worry. I'm going to win the game for you." He was the [second] batter in that inning. First pitch, home run. He won the game for me.

Beating the great Warren Spahn in that game, that was something. It was special. The stadium was almost empty because people didn't stay for the end of the game. It was a night game. But I know in the Dominican, there's a three-hour difference. So over there it was like 4:00 in the morning, and everybody was still awake listening. Oh, yes. It was something.

Brooks Robinson

Brooks Calbert Robinson, Jr.
Born: May 18, 1937, in Little Rock, Arkansas
MLB debut: September 17, 1955
Final game: August 13, 1977
Team: Baltimore Orioles (1955–1977)
Primary position: Third base
Bats: Right—**Throws:** Right
Hall of Fame induction: 1983
Vote: 344 votes of 374 ballots cast, 91.98%

Brooks Robinson established the gold standard for modern-day third basemen, setting major-league records at the position for seasons, with 23; games played, with 2,870; fielding percentage, at .971; putouts, with 2,697; assists, with 6,205; and double plays, with 618. His sterling play at the hot corner earned him the nickname the "Human Vacuum Cleaner."

His 268 career home runs were a record at the time for third basemen, while his 16 Gold Gloves, one every year from 1960 to 1975, are tied for second all-time with pitcher Jim Kaat, two behind pitcher Greg Maddux.

In addition to his spectacular defense, Robinson was also an offensive threat, including his American League MVP season of 1964, hitting .317, second best in the AL, with 28 home runs and a league-best 118 RBIs. The 15-time All-Star—he appeared in 18 All-Star Games, including two each in 1960, 1961, and 1962—finished in the top five in MVP voting in four other seasons and led the league in games played five times, including 1961 (163), 1962 (162), 1963 (161), 1964 (163), and 1968 (162). He was the All-Star Game MVP in 1966, going 3-for-4 with a triple, scoring the AL's only run in a 2–1 10-inning loss to the NL. He had six seasons with 20 or more home runs, including a career-high 28 in 1964.

He also played 25 games at second base and five at shortstop for the O's, committing just one total error at those positions. His 23 seasons with the Orioles are a major-league record for longevity with one team, matching Carl Yastrzemski's tenure with the Red Sox.

Robinson led the O's to World Series championships in 1966 and 1970, when he was named the Series MVP, batting .429 with two home runs and six RBIs in five games, with his usual defensive gems. In Game 1 of the 1970 World Series against the Reds, Robinson hit a go-ahead solo home run in the seventh inning, the eventual game-winner for the O's. One inning earlier he made one of his many fielding jewels, backhanding a sharp grounder from Lee May in foul territory behind third base, making an off-balance, one-hop throw to Boog Powell at first, nailing May.

Overall, in nine postseason series, Robinson hit .303 (44-for-145) with five home runs and 22 RBIs.

Hugely popular during his playing days, Robinson remains a favorite of Orioles fans, many of whom have named their children after him. Royals Hall of Famer George Brett chose uniform No. 5 as a tribute to Robinson, one of his boyhood idols.

In 1999 Robinson was named to Major League Baseball's All-Century Team, and was ranked 80th on *The Sporting News* list of 100 Greatest Baseball Players, and in 2007 was named to the All-Time Gold Glove Team.

In 1966 Brooks fulfilled a childhood dream.

Well, I can tell you it was the final game of the first World Series I played, in 1966. As a youngster growing up I never wanted to do anything else in my life but be a baseball player. You dream about signing a contract, playing in the minor leagues, reaching the major leagues, winning the pennant, getting in the World Series, and winning it. That's all you can ask. And the Orioles had a chance for the World Series in 1960 and didn't quite make it. In 1964 we were a couple of games short. And we finally arrived at the World Series in 1966 and we won four games in a row from the Dodgers. The final game was here in Baltimore, and we won that to become world champions. So that's really the highlight of the games that I can recall. That, to me, is my favorite game.

I remember we'd won three in a row. We won two in California. We beat Don Drysdale. Then we beat Sandy Koufax. Paul Blair hit a home run in the third game, and we won that game 1–0. The next game it was Drysdale pitching against Dave McNally, and we won that game 1–0 when Frank Robinson hit a home run off of Drysdale. But I just remember it was the first World Series that the Orioles—the modern Orioles—had ever been in, and you know how a World Series or Super Bowl brings a city together. And that's exactly what happened in 1966.

It was a day game. The weather was nice. Actually, I played in the first night game in World Series history, too. That was out in Pittsburgh, the fourth game of the World Series in 1971.

But the first game of that World Series in '66 was exciting, too, because I hit a home run the first time up.

Brooks Robinson (No. 5) leaps across the infield to congratulate pitcher Dave McNally (No. 19) and catcher Andy Etchenbarren after the final out in Game 4 of the 1966 World Series on October 9, 1966.

Frank Robinson hit before me and he hit a home run. And then I hit the next pitch for a home run. So hitting a home run the first time in a World Series is pretty exciting. It was just right down the middle. I always kid Frank about it and I say, "Mine went farther than yours." He hit a lot more than I did, but I still say, "Frank, my home run dwarfed your home run." Ah, he just smiles.

The other game that comes back that really stands out was in 1964. We went right down to the wire with the New York Yankees, the White Sox, and the Orioles. The Yankees ended up winning by one game over the White Sox and two against us. But this was [August 22], and I think it was the top of the ninth inning, and Joe Horlen was pitching. We had two runners on, and I hit a three-run homer to win that game, to pull us right even with the

Yankees or one game behind, or whatever [the win put the Orioles one and a half games ahead of the White Sox]. But I hit a three-run homer in the ninth to win the game, and that kind of stands out as a signature game for me.

In '66 it was special. And the thing is, every time I think of one of those guys, because a lot of them have passed away, I get a big smile on my face because it always brings back a great memory of the time we had that year. We were pretty much out in front the whole time. In baseball lingo, we were blowing everyone away. We won by nine games, I think, to win the pennant.

The Dodgers were overwhelming favorites because they had a lot of guys who had already played in a World Series. I think Frank Robinson was maybe the only guy we had who was in the '61 Series, with Cincinnati against the Yankees. But it was a big upset. And I played in four [1966 beating Los Angeles; 1969 losing to the Mets; 1970 beating Cincinnati; and 1971 losing to Pittsburgh]. The two we were supposed to win, we lost. And the two we were supposed to lose, we won. We played against the Mets in 1969 and we were big favorites there. We won the first game and then we lost four in a row. We were underdogs to Cincinnati and we won. Then Pittsburgh we were favored and we lost. You can't explain it.

When we played the Mets, that was probably the best team I ever played on, the 1969 team. We won, like, 109 games [109–53 in the regular season], I think, and we lost our last five out of six during the season. But I think when people thought of the Mets, they thought of the inception of the Mets when they lost 120 games [in 1962] and they were the bumbling fools, you know? But these guys won 100 games. I think people forget that. When you have a Seaver, and a Koosman, and Gentry, they had good pitching. They made some great plays. There were a lot of kind of quirky things that happened. So that was it. But it'd be hard to explain. In the big leagues in the last 10 years, we've had a couple of wild-card teams, like the [Red Sox in 2004], and Florida beat the Yankees a few years ago [in 2003]. So, if you just get a hot team and a couple of hot pitchers, well, you've got a chance to win.

The most famous picture in Orioles history showed me after the final out [of the 1966 World Series], jumping about 10 feet in the air, arriving at the pitcher. That was the exciting part of it. But I think about every guy on that team, and I just get a big smile on my face. We had a little reunion a couple of years ago here in Baltimore. That was really special.

It's bittersweet. Absolutely, it is, thinking back. I think of Dave McNally, who was probably my closest friend on the team, he passed away at age 60, I guess, a couple years ago. Aparicio, he's still living. But there's a group of guys that are not with us now. I haven't seen Wally Bunker in 40 years. There's three or four of the guys that never really come around. They're living somewhere else, and they just don't get back to Baltimore. It was a group here that kind of sponsored everyone coming back. And we had a little get-together and a reunion dinner at Morgan State University, and a lot of people came. Hank Bauer was our manager, who just passed away this past year. The coaches, they've passed, too.

But that was just a great team and a great time.

Luis Aparicio

Luis Ernesto (Montiel) Aparicio
Born: April 29, 1934, in Maracaibo, Venezuela
MLB debut: April 17, 1956
Final game: September 28, 1973
Teams: Chicago White Sox (1956–1962, 1968–1970),
    Baltimore Orioles (1963–1967), Boston Red Sox
    (1971–1973)
Primary position: Shortstop
Bats: Right—**Throws:** Right
Hall of Fame induction: 1984
Vote: 341 votes of 403 ballots cast, 84.62%

Fast and agile, Luis Aparicio was as much a threat on the base paths as he was at shortstop. Playing in 152 games in 1956, Aparicio was named American League Rookie of the Year, hitting .266 and leading the league with 21 stolen bases against just four times caught, for an 84 percent success rate. A 10-time All-Star in his 18-year career, Aparicio collected nine Gold Gloves and led the American League in stolen bases for nine consecutive seasons, from 1956 to 1964. With 506 career stolen bases, Aparicio posted a 79 percent success rate.

Aparicio, the first South American inducted into the Hall of Fame, helped to define slick-fielding, spray-hitting, base-stealing shortstops. That was the only position he played in his 2,601 career games, posting a .972 fielding percentage. Upon his retirement in 1973, he held the record for games

Luis Aparicio throws the ball over Kansas City's Jim Landis to complete a double play in the seventh inning of this July 23, 1965, game in Baltimore.

played at shortstop, until Omar Vizquel passed that mark in May 2008. "Little Looie" also established since-broken shortstop records for assists, with 8,016; chances, with 12,564; and double plays, with 1,553. With second baseman Nellie Fox, he formed one of the slickest double-play combos in baseball history. Aparicio had the most American League putouts by a shortstop, with 4,548, and led the league in fielding eight times.

In 1959, although he hit just .257 with six home runs and 51 RBIs, he led the league with 56 stolen bases, scoring 98 runs, and finishing second in MVP voting to teammate Fox.

In 1959 Aparicio helped the White Sox to the World Series, though they fell to the Dodgers despite Aparicio's .308 (8-for-26) hitting. But Aparicio would get his revenge against Los Angeles, helping the Orioles to the 1966 World Series championship over the Dodgers in his final postseason appearance.

While Aparicio had thousands of games to choose from, it was a particular game in New York that stood out as his favorite—but not for an on-field accomplishment.

I think my favorite game was in New York because that was where I met my wife. It really was. It was one I can't forget. When you have so many games, they all seem the same, and sometimes you play better than other times. But I remember that particular game because I met my wife at Yankee Stadium. She is Jim Rivera's cousin. Jim used to play for the White Sox. Then after the ballgame we went to a restaurant in New York. The name of the restaurant was El Rancho. I think it was on 42nd Street or something like that. And he introduced me to her, and six months later we were married, and she's still with me. So how could I forget that game?

Harmon Killebrew

Harmon Clayton Killebrew
Born: June 29, 1936, in Payette, Idaho
MLB debut: June 23, 1954
Final game: September 26, 1975
Teams: Washington Senators (1954–1960), Minnesota Twins
    (1961–1974), Kansas City Royals (1975)
Primary position: First base
Bats: Right—**Throws:** Right
Hall of Fame induction: 1984
Vote: 335 votes of 403 ballots cast, 83.13%

At the conclusion of his 22-year career, Harmon Killebrew
was second only to Babe Ruth in American League home
runs with 573, and was the career leader in home runs by a
right-handed hitter. His 393 home runs in the 1960s were the
most in that decade.

Killebrew signed with the Washington Senators on June
19, 1954, after Idaho senator Herman Welker recommended
the slugger to Senators owner Clark Griffith. Four days later—
and six days before his 18th birthday—Killebrew made his
major-league debut, the youngest player in the major leagues
at the time.

As a "bonus baby," Killebrew played in just 113 games
in his first five seasons, hitting 11 home runs in 254 at-bats
in that stretch. But in 1959 he established himself as one of
the most dangerous hitters in the league, hitting 42 roundtrippers, the first of his eight 40-plus home-run seasons.

Killebrew, whose nickname "Killer" was in stark contrast to his quiet, respectful demeanor, led the league in home runs in 1959 (42), 1962 (48), 1963 (45), 1964 (49), 1967 (44), and 1969 (49); RBIs in 1962 (126), 1969 (140), and 1971 (119); walks in 1966 (103), 1967 (131), 1969 (145), and 1971 (114); intentional walks in 1966 (18), 1967 (15), and 1969 (20); at-bats-to-home-runs ratio in 1959, (13.0), 1962 (11.5), 1963 (11.4), 1967 (12.4), 1969 (11.3), and 1970 (12.9); on-base percentage in 1969 (.427); and slugging percentage in 1963 (.555).

Killebrew was named the AL MVP in 1969, batting .276 with 49 home runs and 140 RBIs; slugging .584, with a .427 on-base percentage; and playing 162 games. He finished in the top five in MVP voting in an additional five seasons. An 11-time All-Star, Killebrew hit .308 with three home runs and six RBIs in 11 Midsummer Classics. In 1999 Killebrew was ranked No. 69 on *The Sporting News* list of 100 Greatest Baseball Players.

The powerful Killebrew averaged one home run every 14.2 at-bats in his career. His 520-foot, three-run homer to the upper deck in left-center field on June 3, 1967, against Lew Burdette and the Angels is the longest ever hit at Metropolitan Stadium. He is also one of just four sluggers—with Frank Howard, Cecil Fielder, and Mark McGwire—to reach the left-field roof of old Tiger Stadium.

It's not surprising, then, that the first and last of his 573 career home runs are memorable.

———————————

I can tell you about the first home run I hit, which was pretty special to me. I signed when I was 17 and I was with the old Washington Senators for about half a year, and I didn't hit a home run that first go with the Senators.

And the next year I turned 18, and we were playing against the Detroit Tigers in old Griffith Stadium in Washington [June 24, 1955, a year and a day after his major-league debut]. They had a veteran left-handed pitcher on the mound by the name of Billy Hoeft, and the catcher was a veteran catcher by the name of Frank House. And when I stepped in the batter's box, Frank House said, "Kid, we're going to throw you a fastball." He called me kid! I was so young and naïve I didn't know whether he was telling me the truth or not. But sure enough, there it was. And I hit it 476 feet. As I came around the bases and touched home plate, he said, "Hey, kid, that's the last time we're ever going to tell you what's coming." And it was. Nobody ever said it after that.

I don't know what he was thinking, whether he was trying to confuse me, tell me a fastball and he throws a curve or something. But that's certainly something I'll never forget, because that was my first home run in the major leagues.

When I think back to that day, it's crystal clear. I remember everything: what he said to me, running around the bases, touching home plate, and then what he said. That was a neat thing. Every one of them was, though, to tell you truth. I remember the first one and the last one and quite a few in between.

The last one, well, I was with the Kansas City Royals my last year. I had played 21 years with the same organization, the Griffith organization, and then I went to Kansas City my last year, and I hit my last home run against the Minnesota Twins in Minnesota [September 18, 1975] off a young pitcher by the name of Eddie Bane, a little left-hander we had. So that was a different feeling for me. It was bittersweet. Yeah, it was. Someone said, "Why'd you hit it off Eddie Bane?" I said, "Well, I didn't know it would be my last home run!"

But over the years there were so many things, and it's hard to pinpoint one when you've played as long as I did. There's a lot of things come to mind. I think it's every ballplayer's dream to play in the World Series. It certainly was mine, to play against the Dodgers in 1965 and hit against Koufax. That was a memorable game, the last game of the World Series that year. Koufax pitched against us. He shut us out, 2–0, with two days' rest. I got the last hit off him in that game. So that one I'll always remember. I got a hit. There was two out. Bob Allison was the last hitter in the game. He came up and he struck out. He took his bat and hit it on the ground and broke it. And I told him—Bob and I roomed together for 10 years—I said, "Bob, if you'd have swung at the ball as hard as you swung at the ground, we might have won the game."

But Koufax, that was the greatest game I ever saw pitched. Throwing with two days' rest, throwing mostly fastballs. His control was just pinpoint perfect. That was a memorable thing.

I was very apprehensive about playing in Minnesota, when the team moved from Washington. I played parts of seven years in Washington with the Senators, and there were so many neat things in the nation's capital. One day President Eisenhower came out to the ballpark, June of 1959. They called me over. He wanted to get an autographed ball from me for his grandson David. That was something. It was a great thrill. And I said, "Mr. President, I'll give you one, but will you give me one in return?" Of course, I wasn't going to refuse anything he wanted to do. But he gave me an autograph on a baseball, and I still have it. There were so many things like that in the nation's capital.

Hitting a home run in the World Series, one off Drysdale. Home runs in All-Star Games. On my first home run, rounding the bases, I wasn't really nervous, no. But I probably ran around there fast! It was in June. I think it was June 24. I've got it written down somewhere.

A lot of years had gone by after that first home run, so it was kind of a different feeling on my last home run. I was so young when I hit my first one—only 18—and then I was 39 when I hit my last one.

Lou Brock

Louis Clark Brock
Born: June 18, 1939, in El Dorado, Arkansas
MLB debut: September 10, 1961
Final game: September 30, 1979
Teams: Chicago Cubs (1961–1964), St. Louis Cardinals
    (1964–1979)
Primary position: Left field
Bats: Left—**Throws:** Left
Hall of Fame induction: 1985
Vote: 315 votes of 395 ballots cast, 79.75%

Lou Brock revolutionized base stealing, leading the National League in thefts in eight of his 19 seasons. He retired as the all-time stolen-base leader with 938 steals against 307 times caught for a 75 percent success rate.

Brock was signed by the Cubs in 1960, making his major-league debut late in the next season. But after two less-than-impressive seasons, he was sent to the Cardinals in 1964 in a six-player trade, essentially Brock for Ernie Broglio, Cubs fans have long held that it was the worst trade in the team's history.

Brock blossomed with the Cardinals. That season he hit .348 with 12 home runs, 44 RBIs, and 33 stolen bases in 103 games for the Cardinals, helping them to the first of their three World Series appearances—and two championships—in his time in St. Louis. In 21 World Series games, Brock hit .391 with four home runs, 13 RBIs, and 14 stolen bases.

In addition to his stolen-base titles, he was a six-time All-Star, and in 1967 was the first player to hit 20 home runs and steal 50 bases in a season. He had more than 50 stolen bases in 12 consecutive seasons. Brock finished his career with 3,023 hits, a .293 average, and 149 home runs. He hit over .300 eight times and led the National League in runs in 1967 (113) and 1971 (126); doubles in 1968 (46); triples in 1968 (14); and singles in 1972 (156).

His career and single-season (118 swipes in 1974) records for stolen bases were both eventually broken by Rickey Henderson. But the National League honors the season leader in stolen bases each year with the Lou Brock Award.

Despite his success on the base paths, it was a game that taught him to harness his speed that he remembers the most.

Oh, I don't know, I had a few favorites, I guess, nothing tops 3,000 hits, and I had a lot of good World Series games, a lot of seasons like that. But that moment in itself is like the crowning of a career.

I guess the game that stands out in my mind would be in Philadelphia, probably in September of 1964. It was a game we were trailing [5–3]. I was trying to stretch a single into a double, got caught in a rundown, got out of the rundown. We were [two runs] down when I tried all of that. I got out of the rundown, and we actually won the game. I guess I remember it mostly because it *saved* me. Being able to get out of the rundown and eventually win the game and eventually win the pennant by one game. That was probably the game I remember most. We wound up winning the game and winning the pennant

Lou Brock steals his 55ᵗʰ base of the season with a head-first slide in the eighth inning of the August 31, 1965, game against the Cubs in Chicago.

that year. That was my greatest game and my greatest memory.

I'd been caught many times before in a rundown, but never in the ninth inning when the ballclub was trailing by [two runs]. It was really late in the game, ninth inning. Top of the ninth, down [two runs], one out. You get a base hit and now you're in a rundown. I don't know why I tried to stretch it. They had a shortstop by the name of Cookie Rojas who really played second base. They had put him in center field. And I always thought an infielder had no reason, no right, to be in the outfield. So we were going to teach them a lesson because they put a second baseman in center field. So that's what happened.

His arm didn't surprise me. I knew he could throw. But sometimes when a guy is out of position, his thinking is sometimes also in disarray. But in this case he wasn't. I was the guy who was in disarray. But I think that was a big reason. And it was a close play. I finally got back to first base, and the first baseman missed the tag, and I got a reprieve. I never talked to him about that play afterward. Oh, no, I didn't even want to bring it up to anyone. I just wanted it to go away. I was afraid other people would remember. But I remember.

I didn't have a reputation then. I was establishing one. I was a guy who walked on the edge a little bit. You could walk in the middle and make no error or you could walk on the edge and be outstanding. But when you walk on the edge and you're not outstanding on any particular day, then there are some problems.

Somebody asked me why I tried to stretch a single into a double, and I thought about it. Cookie Rojas, the infielder, had been put in center field. And he didn't have what we call an outfield arm. When you're up against a guy who doesn't have an outfield arm, you take chances. So I took a chance, and I almost blew the whole championship.

Oh, I was in five or six throws, between the first baseman and second baseman, and I was coming back to first base. The first baseman tagged high, I went low, and the umpire said "safe." That was it. It's probably the greatest rundown I ever got out of. It saved my skin. I'd gotten out of other rundowns before, but never in that kind of situation. Early in the game you take chances and do those things. But with a second baseman playing center field, and he doesn't have an outfield arm, you would take a little more risk. I made a risky move and I almost paid for it.

Bobby Doerr

Robert Pershing Doerr
Born: April 7, 1918, in Los Angeles, California
MLB debut: April 20, 1937
Final game: September 7, 1951
Team: Boston Red Sox (1937–1944, 1946–1951)
Primary position: Second base
Bats: Right—**Throws:** Right
Hall of Fame induction: 1986
Vote: Elected to the Hall of Fame by the Veterans Committee

Bobby Doerr was signed by the Red Sox on the same scouting trip that put Ted Williams into a Boston uniform. Doerr debuted as a 19-year-old and played no other position but second base in his 14-year career. A true gentleman, he would become the team's "silent captain," as Williams called him.

He was named The Sporting News American League Player of the Year in 1944. But he missed the 1945 season, serving in the army during World War II. Returning in 1946, Doerr hit .271 with 18 home runs and 116 RBIs, finishing third in MVP voting—won by Williams—and helping the Sox reach the World Series, when he hit .409 in Boston's seven-game loss to the Cardinals, his only postseason play.

He led AL second basemen in double plays five times, tying a record; in putouts and fielding percentage four times; and in assists three times.

A chronic back ailment led to his retirement after the 1951 season at the age of 33.

Upon his retirement, he had the major-league record for career double plays for second basemen, with 1,507, and fielding percentage at .980. In 1948 he set an AL record, handling 414 consecutive chances at second base over 73 games without an error.

Doerr led the league in slugging percentage in 1944 (.528); games played in 1943 (155); triples in 1950 (11); and sacrifices in 1938 (22).

A nine-time All-Star, Bobby drove in over 100 runs in six seasons. In 1,865 games in his 14-season career, he hit .288 with 2,042 hits, 223 home runs, 1,247 RBIs, 381 doubles, and 89 triples. At Fenway Park he hit .315 with 145 home runs.

With so many All-Star Games on his résumé, it's no wonder he has fond memories for one particular Midsummer Classic.

Well, there are two or three games that kind of stand out. I suppose the 1943 All-Star Game where I hit the home run and we ended up winning, I think, 5–3, would have been one of the games that would have been a memory for me. It was in the second inning or so, and two men on. Mort Cooper was pitching. He threw me a high, hanging curveball that I remember hitting for a home run in Shibe Park in Philadelphia. That was the first night game ever played for an All-Star Game. That was quite a pleasant memory. Then, I think the [second] time up or something against Vander Meer I got a base hit. I got two hits in that All-Star Game. It was a curveball, and what was interesting was that I remember very plainly that we played Cincinnati a lot in spring training, and I remember several times when he would get 3–2, most of the time back in those days you'd pretty much get a fastball on 3–2. And he most every time would give you a curveball. So I didn't really guess much on hitting ever. I always was hitting off of the fastball. But this time I was just definitely looking for a curveball, 3–2, and he threw me a curveball, and I got a base hit by the third baseman. But I remember that very vividly because of the past play in spring training. That was one of the games that would be a fond memory.

In Philadelphia it was a good night. Joe McCarthy was managing, and he didn't have a Yankee player in the lineup that night. That was unusual. And we still beat the National League in that game.

We weren't playing a whole lot of night games then. The All-Star Games had just started about 10 years before. And I guess things you did in All-Star Games or World Series were always great thrills. I think back then All-Star Games were magnified a little bit more. It wasn't just another game. It was something you really wanted to be in and you wanted to win pretty badly. I think bragging rights counted more back then if you beat the other league. I remember Ted Williams being in it. He was all up. Back then it seemed like there was more verbal stuff on the bench, yelling at the other team and stuff like that. I remember Ted yelling a little bit, yelling about wanting to win and stuff.

And I suppose the other game, I don't know what year that was, 1948, '49, '50, in there [1950]. Well, we beat St. Louis [29–4] or something. I got three home runs and drove in, I think, eight runs in that game. But those would be games that I remember fondly.

Most of the times when it would amount to anything, you would remember pretty much which pitch you hit. I remember getting my 2,000th hit at Yankee Stadium. I think it was July 1, 1951. Lopat was pitching, and Lopat was kind of a junkball pitcher, an off- and on-speed type. And, in later years, I got to where I hit him more to the opposite field and had better luck with him. I remember he threw a ball, it was kind of a sinking outside fastball. And I hit it into right field for my 2,000th hit. And Yogi Berra was catching. He ran out past the pitcher and got the ball and tossed it to me over at first base. I thought that was very thoughtful of him.

There were games like that—where we didn't win the game—but that last game in '49 where we got beat by the Yankees, that was a very memorable game. I remember I hit a triple in that game. We came within a run or so of getting up, and that's when [Jerry] Coleman hit the bloop triple into right field that put them ahead. That was a memorable game, not that I did anything so great in it. But we were a game in front with two games to play. We played in Washington and we came back to New York with a game lead. Then they beat us on Saturday and they beat us again on Sunday.

I played in the first All-Star Game in 1941, and I think the only one I missed after that was in '49. I had a lousy start that year. In fact, on June 15, 1949, I think I was hitting about .215 and, oh, I was terrible. It was the worst start I'd ever had playing ball. It was just, gosh, you didn't know what the heck was going on. I remember Birdie Tebbetts saying, "Bobby, you should see about getting your eyes checked." Well, I thought about that a lot, wondering. And, boy, I went. I had a doctor friend set up for me to get my eyes checked. The eye doctor said, "Oh, your eyes are real good."

Back in those days, when you got in those kinds of ruts, you went out and took extra batting practice, try this and try that, and different stances. I remember backing off the plate sometime in the middle of June. Where I was pretty much a pull hitter, in the minor leagues I was pretty much straightaway, right-center, left-center, center field. And when I backed away from the plate, it made everything outside on you. And I started hitting everything to center field and right field, and from June 15 to the end of the season I hit .350. Everything was going good. I was hitting .215 and I ended up hitting .309. So those were pleasant memories of the last half of that season.

In 1947 was another All-Star Game that would be memorable. We were playing at Wrigley Field, and I didn't play the first half of that game, I went in the second half. I think it was the [seventh] inning. Johnny Sain was pitching. It was tough to see in that ballpark in the daytime because it was white shirts all around. And I remember he threw me two curveballs that I just got flashes of. It just seemed like, man, it was impossible to hit it because you didn't hardly see it. And then he was going to waste a fastball on me, which pitchers generally do to break things up a little bit. And he threw me a fastball, and it must have been eight, 10 inches over my head. I saw that. It looked like a balloon compared to the other pitches. I hit it for a base hit into left field. And Buddy Rosar was batting, and he put a hit-and-run on with me. But he missed the ball. I stole second base. And then Sain tried to pick me off second. He hit me in the back with the ball. The ball went into center field and I went to third base. And then Stan Spence was the next hitter and he got a base hit to drive me in, and we won that game 2–1.

In that game, it was interesting. Kind of one of those things that only I knew what had happened. I think it was in the last of the [eighth] inning. The National League had a man on base with two outs, and Enos Slaughter was the hitter, and he hit a big hopper over the pitcher's head, just barely on my side of second base. I was playing pretty deep because, with two outs, you didn't want the ball to get by you. And when it was hit, it was just one of those things, a miracle if you throw him out. Just as I was going to field the ball, Boudreau came over in front of me to field the ball and just barely got Slaughter out at first base, or that would have been the tying run.

There are a lot of pleasant memories, just being able to play baseball. I look back at how fortunate I was to be able to play with great players like we had, Foxx and Cronin and Ted Williams, Dom DiMaggio, Pesky, those great players for the Red Sox. And it made you a better ballplayer, no question about it, by having good players around you.

Willie McCovey

Willie Lee McCovey
Born: January 10, 1938, in Mobile, Alabama
MLB debut: July 30, 1959
Final game: July 6, 1980
Teams: San Francisco Giants (1959–1973, 1977–1980), San
  Diego Padres (1974–1976), Oakland A's (1976)
Primary position: First base
Bats: Left—**Throws:** Left
Hall of Fame induction: 1986
Vote: 346 votes of 425 ballots cast, 81.41%

After debuting as a 21-year-old, Willie McCovey played 22 seasons, leaving an indelible mark on baseball. A six-time All-Star, he was the National League MVP in 1969, when he hit .320 with 45 home runs and 126 RBIs.

McCovey finished his career hitting .270 with 521 home runs and 1,555 RBIs. He led the league in on-base percentage in 1969 (.453); slugging percentage in 1968 (.545), 1969 (.656), and 1970 (.612); home runs in 1963 (44), 1968 (36), and 1969 (45); at-bats-per-home-runs in 1963 (12.8), 1967 (14.7), 1968 (14.5), 1969 (10.9), and 1970 (12.7); RBIs in 1968 (105) and 1969 (126); walks in 1970 (137); intentional walks in 1969 (45), 1970 (40), 1971 (21), and 1973 (25); and on base in 1970 (283).

Upon his retirement, his home-run total was the best mark for left-handed hitters in the National League—eventually passed by Barry Bonds—and he was second only to Lou

Gehrig, with a National League–record 18 career grand slams. McCovey, Ted Williams (who finished their careers with the same number of home runs), and Rickey Henderson are the only players to homer in four decades. Willie's 236 career home runs at Candlestick Park were more than anyone else hit there.

The game that started it all and led to his Rookie of the Year campaign in 1959, when he hit .354 with 13 home runs and 38 RBIs, slugging .656 in just 52 games, stands out for McCovey.

———————

O h, I had so many. My very first game [July 30, 1959] when I went 4-for-4 [with two triples, three runs scored, and two RBIs] against Robin Roberts. It's hard to top that. And of course you remember the big ones, like what you did in All-Star Games and things like that. The 1969 All-Star Game in Washington, I hit two home runs and was the MVP of that game. And you always remember your milestones, like your 500th home run and things like that.

In that very first game I was a young fresh kid just coming up to the major leagues. I was very nervous. Once the game started, though, I was okay. But, yeah, I was nervous as heck. I was having a great year in Triple A when they called me up. We had just played a doubleheader the night before in Phoenix, so I was up all night. I didn't get any sleep. So I was playing on just fumes, no sleep at all, and still went 4-for-4. So that was all right.

I didn't know anything about Robin Roberts. Just that I had read about him a lot and I had seen a lot of the games on TV when he and [Don] Newcombe used to hook up. They was always 1–0, 2–0, 2–1 games. I used to like to watch those matches when Newcombe and Roberts pitched against each other. So I knew who he was, not necessarily what to look for. I just knew that he was a great pitcher. But Mays filled me in on what pitchers threw my first time around the league because he had faced them before. But that first game was a good one.

Billy Williams

Billy Leo Williams
Born: June 15, 1938, in Whistler, Alabama
MLB debut: August 6, 1959
Final game: October 2, 1976
Teams: Chicago Cubs (1959–1974), Oakland A's (1975–1976)
Primary position: Left field
Bats: Left—**Throws:** Right
Hall of Fame induction: 1987
Vote: 354 votes of 413 ballots cast, 85.71%

After signing with the Cubs as an amateur free agent, Billy Williams, "Sweet Swingin' Billy from Whistler," was named the National League Rookie of the Year in 1961, hitting .278 with 25 home runs and 86 RBIs in 146 games. In 1972 he was named The Sporting News Player of the Year, when he hit .333 with 37 home runs and 122 RBIs in 150 games. His Rookie of the Year season was the first of 13 consecutive seasons in which Williams had at least 20 home runs and 80 RBIs.

In 18 seasons, Williams was chosen for six All-Star teams. Upon his retirement after the 1976 season, Williams finished with a .290 average, 2,711 hits, and 1,475 RBIs in 2,488 games.

He held the National League record for consecutive games played, with 1,117 from September 22, 1963, through September 2, 1970, until he was eventually passed by Steve Garvey. Williams set NL marks for games played by an outfielder in one season, with 164 in 1965. He also set an NL record with nine consecutive seasons of 600 or more at-bats from 1962 through 1970, a mark that was eventually broken by Pete Rose.

Williams tied major-league records with five home runs in back-to-back games on September 8 and September 10, 1968, and with four straight doubles in a game on April 9, 1969.

He led the league in batting average in 1972, with a .333 clip; in slugging percentage in 1972 (.606); games played in 1965 (164), 1966 (162), 1968 (163), 1969 (163), and 1970 (161); runs scored in 1970 (137); hits in 1970 (205); total bases in 1968 (321), 1970 (373), and 1972 (348); and extra-base hits in 1965 (79), 1968 (68), and 1972 (77).

On June 29, 1969, the Cubs celebrated Billy Williams Day at Wrigley Field in a doubleheader against the St. Louis Cardinals. Honoring the man who broke Stan Musial's National League record of 896 consecutive games played, the Cubs swept the Cards 3–1 and 12–1 in the twin bill. In the two games, Williams went a combined 5-for-9 with two doubles, two triples, four runs scored, and three RBIs.

It's easy to see why that day stands out for Sweet Swingin' Billy.

It was a game we played in 1969. Of course, the whole year was exciting, and in 1969 when we played a doubleheader in Chicago, it was set aside as Billy Williams Day, June 29. And that day we were playing the St. Louis Cardinals and we beat them in a doubleheader. And along with that, just the whole year was exciting. That particular day I got about five hits, and the last time at the plate I was hitting for a home run. I was swinging

Chicago Cubs outfielder Billy Williams at spring training in 1968.

for a home run for the cycle, and I wound up striking out. And the 40,000 people in the ballpark and the 10,000 that couldn't get in, they start cheering. So it was one of the first times a guy ever got cheered for striking out! But it was an exciting day.

It was a day that was named Billy Williams Day because they liked to appreciate those players who had done a great job for the organization. And, of course, Ernie [Banks] had a day in Chicago. And Santo had a day in Chicago. And of course I had my day on June 29. So it was a great day.

That's been quite a while ago. I don't know if I remember who the pitchers were. I think Bob Gibson was the first pitcher in the first game, because normally when Bob Gibson was pitching, Fergie was pitching. Against Gibson I did, well, fair. Well, we had our confrontations. He got me out. I got a couple of base hits that day, I think [1-for-4]. That first game was a quick game, and I'm glad, because we had two games to play. [Dick Selma and Mudcat Grant] pitched in the second ballgame. And we beat the Cardinals in a doubleheader.

Red Schoendienst

Albert Fred Schoendienst
Born: February 2, 1923, in Germantown, Illinois
MLB debut: April 17, 1945
Final game: July 7, 1963
Teams: St. Louis Cardinals (1945–1956, 1961–1963), New
 York Giants (1956–1957), Milwaukee Braves (1957–1960)
Primary position: Second base
Bats: Switch—**Throws:** Right
Hall of Fame induction: 1989
Vote: Elected to the Hall of Fame by the Veterans Committee

Signed by the Cardinals as an amateur free agent in 1942, Schoendienst made his debut as a 22-year-old left fielder in 1945, playing 118 games in the outfield, 10 at shortstop, and just one at second base—where he would ultimately find his home—and led the National League with 26 stolen bases.

In his 19 seasons (17 full seasons), Schoendienst led the National League in fielding percentage six times, including 1956 when he set a league record at .9934, eventually surpassed by Ryne Sandberg in 1986. In 1950 Red went 57 consecutive games and a record 323 straight chances without an error.

The 10-time All-Star hit .289 with 2,449 hits, 84 home runs, 773 RBIs, and 1,223 runs scored in 2,216 games over his career. At second base he fielded .983 over his career, with 4,616 putouts, 5,243 assists, 1,368 double plays, and just 170 errors in 10,029 total chances. He hit .300 or better in seven seasons.

His fourteenth-inning home run—and first career homer batting right-handed—won the 1950 All-Star Game for the National League (a highlight for Ralph Kiner).

Arguably, his finest season was 1953, when he hit .342, second in the league by two percentage points to Brooklyn's Carl Furillo, with 15 home runs and 79 RBIs.

He won the 1946 World Series with the Cardinals and the 1957 World Series and 1958 National League pennant with the Braves.

Tuberculosis limited him to just five games in 1959, but he returned in 1960, hitting .257 with a home run and 19 RBIs in 68 games. In 1961 he returned to the Cardinals as a player/coach, hitting .300 in 72 games. Since then he has served the Cardinals as coach, and manager—winning the 1967 World Series at the helm—and is still a special assistant to the general manager.

Schoendienst led the league in at-bats in 1947 (659) and 1950 (642); hits in 1957 (200); doubles in 1950 (43); stolen bases in 1945 (26); singles in 1949 (160); sacrifices in 1950 (16); and at-bats per strikeout in 1949 (35.6) and 1957 (43.2).

One of the most popular figures in Cardinals and St. Louis baseball history, Schoendienst has spent parts of the last seven decades in a Cardinals uniform.

It's no wonder one of his fondest memories is the game that started it all.

———————————

W ell, it's hard to choose. There are so many great memories. Especially when you're first starting out. I was signed to a minor-league club, and the first game I ever played was in D ball. And the Cardinals at that time had three or four D teams alone. There were over 500 minor-league players. They'd sign you to a contract and they didn't see you other than to work out back then. And you're a little nervous. It's your first game out there, and everybody's watching you. And you're hoping you do good, or hoping you don't get sent home if you don't do good. You and your poppy did.

That was a big thing, my first game. I guess I was 19 years old. My first game was in, I think it was, Lynchburg, Virginia, if I'm not mistaken [Union City, Tennessee]. I don't remember the team name, I just remember they gave me a uniform to play and that was it. But that was a big thing for me, just to be signed to a professional contract and going in and playing and hoping you do well. And I did. I got three or four hits that first ballgame and made a couple of errors. Well, I guess I was a little nervous.

And then Branch Rickey was there. He was the general manager for the Cardinals. And like I said, I made a couple of errors. After that ballgame, he called me over. "Young man," he said, "you made a few errors. Before you get out of this game, you're going to make a few more errors." So he tried to make me feel good. And I did.

I didn't last long down there. I played the rest of that year, that half year. It was July when they signed me. Then the next year I went to B team for spring training. That was my first full year. And then I went right up to Triple A and played for the Rochester ballclub. In fact, I led the league in hitting that first year. And the next year I went in the service for one year, and then I joined the Cardinals in 1945.

So I remember a lot of games. There are so many of them and so many good memories—playing my first World

Red Schoendienst ends up on top of Johnny Pesky while trying to avoid him during Game 6 of the World Series in St. Louis, Missouri, on October 13, 1946.

Series, playing my first professional ball. And every year the season would start, and I always felt a little nervous until the first pitch. It seemed like everything was over with after the first pitch. But I had the nerves every year. All the time. Until the first pitch was thrown, and after that, it was over.

But that's the way it was. Your big games, you go to spring training, they get themselves in great shape so they can win the pennant and the World Series. So that's the way I looked at it. You're here for spring training. You give up a lot of things. But you go out there and play hard. So during the season you're in good shape and you may go to the World Series. I was pretty fortunate. I went to a few of them, anyway.

I don't remember the kids that were on that first team. I can't remember if they ever went to the big leagues or not. But I do know that the manager who was there was from Kirkwood, Missouri, and his name was Everett Johnson. In those days, you were the manager, the bus driver, the traveling secretary, and the trainer. You had to do everything. You pitched batting practice, and you filled in, in case somebody got hurt. You'd fill in. That was a big thing. You didn't have much practice time in those days because you had about 15 ballplayers on each team. You had, I think, one extra player between the outfield, and the infield, and the catcher, and then you had a few pitchers. I think all together they had 18 ballplayers. So you played every day.

He wasn't a tough manager; he just managed the ballclub and kept us in line and told us what to do. He'd coach third base and one of the pitchers or somebody would be at first base. It was a little different than it is today.

I played for 19 years and I managed for 12 years. So I had a lot of fun, a lot of fond memories. And there's not much left after you do all that, other than the Hall of Fame. And I guess I'd have to say that was it. When they put me in the Hall of Fame, I guess I'd done just about everything there is in baseball. It was a lot of fun.

This is about my 65th year or so. I've had a great run. Plus, my kids all love the game of baseball, my wife loved it, my family loved baseball. That's all we did. That's about all there was during the Depression. Wasn't too much going on, and no money to do anything else.

Carl Yastrzemski

Carl Michael Yastrzemski
Born: August 22, 1939, in Southampton, New York
MLB debut: April 11, 1961
Final game: October 2, 1983
Team: Boston Red Sox (1961–1983)
Primary position: Left field
Bats: Left—**Throws:** Right
Hall of Fame induction: 1989
Vote: 423 votes of 447 ballots cast, 94.63%

Carl Yastrzemski debuted as a 21-year-old left fielder, replacing the legendary Ted Williams. That was the first of his career 3,308 games—second all-time to Pete Rose, the most in the American League. That game began a 23-year career with the Red Sox, the only team for which Yaz ever played, tied with Brooks Robinson for the longest tenure in major-league history with one team.

Upon his retirement, Yaz ranked third all-time in at-bats (11,988) and walks (1,845); sixth in total bases (5,539), in hits (3,419), and in doubles (646); and ninth in RBIs (1,844). He was the first American League player with 3,000 hits and 400 home runs (Cal Ripken joined him in 2000).

In two World Series appearances, 1967 and 1975, although the Red Sox didn't win, Yaz hit a combined .352 with three home runs and nine RBIs in 14 games.

Yaz led the AL in batting in 1963 (.321), 1967 (.326), and 1968 (.301); on-base percentage in 1963 (.418), 1965

Carl Yastrzemski hits his second home run off St. Louis Cardinals pitcher Joe Hoerner in the seventh inning of Game 2 of the 1967 World Series at Fenway Park on October 5,1967.

(.395), 1967 (.418), 1968 (.426), and 1970 (.452); slugging percentage in 1965 (.536), 1967 (.622), and 1970 (.592); games played in 1969 (162); runs scored in 1967 (112), 1970 (125), and 1974 (93); hits in 1963 (183) and 1967 (189); total bases in 1967 (360) and 1970 (335); doubles in 1963 (40), 1965 (45), and 1966 (39); home runs in 1967 (44); RBIs in 1967 (121); walks in 1963 (95) and 1968 (119); extra-base hits in 1967 (79); and times on base in 1963 (279), 1967 (284), 1968 (283), and 1970 (315).

A seven-time Gold Glove winner, Yaz hit .285 with 452 home runs over his career. In 14 All-Star Games he hit .294 with one home run—a three-run shot off Tom Seaver in the

1975 Midsummer Classic for the AL's only runs—and five RBIs. He was chosen the 1967 MVP, hitting .326, with 44 home runs and 121 RBIs, missing being a unanimous choice by only one vote.

He was also the Triple Crown winner in 1967, the last batter to accomplish the feat. In 1999 Yaz was ranked No. 72 on *The Sporting News* list of 100 Greatest Baseball Players.

In 1966 the Red Sox finished in ninth place, a half game ahead of the last-place Yankees. In the final 39 games of the 1967 season, Yaz hit .350 with 13 home runs and 31 RBIs. On October 1, 1967, the last game of the season with first place in the American League on the line, Yaz went 4-for-4 with two RBIs and one run scored, and he threw out Bob Allison trying to stretch a single into a double to end the eighth inning, as the Sox defeated the Twins 5–3, capping their "Impossible Dream" season.

I'd have to say the last game of the 1967 season was my favorite. I had many great games and a lot of memories, but that game in particular is special because it was our first pennant, and we were losers in my first six years with the Red Sox. That last game made us winners.

I remember making an error and letting a run score. So I think Minnesota went up 2–0 at the time. And I was just hoping I would have a chance to redeem myself. And then I came up with the bases loaded in the sixth inning, or whatever it was, with the base hit that tied the game up. And then the rally in the eighth inning, throwing out Allison at second base for the third out. They had a rally going, and Harmon Killebrew scored on Allison's hit. So those two things stand out. And I prided myself on defense as well as offense. So that game kind of fit both offense and defense into it.

Dean Chance was pitching for the Twins. He'd won 20 games, something like that. Well, a 20-game winner, you're not going to overwhelm him. Put it that way. He was very tough on right-handed hitters and he was even tough on left-handed hitters. The ball ran away from you. And he threw hard; a hard, heavy sinker. I think I went 4-for-4 that day. So I did alright that day.

It's very difficult to play baseball when you don't have a good team. People don't understand that. I can always remember the last four weeks of that 1967 season. The press was all over the place, and everyone was asking us, "How do you handle the pressure?" Well, when you're playing for the pennant and you're on a good team, there's no pressure. My first six years with the Red Sox, finishing last or next to last, now that's pressure. Because now the fans aren't coming out to see you as a team. They're coming out to watch an individual performance, whereas in 1967, that changed everything, especially the second half of the season. Now, they're coming out to watch the team perform. You can get a standing ovation by making a defensive play. You could get an ovation by starting an inning off with a walk. So it's completely different and it's much easier to play when you're playing for a winner.

I remember the outfield was wet. I don't remember for what reason, but it was very soft. The ball that I made an error on just slowed down. So that's the only reason that it sticks into my memory that the outfield was soggy. In fact, when I threw Allison out at second base, I was over on the left-field line where I used the track and not the outfield grass. I was on the warning track. In fact, I pushed off the box seats because the seats were so close to the line. I used that as leverage to throw to second base.

You know what, I didn't even think about winning the Triple Crown that year. You're so focused on a pennant race and the first pennant. I didn't know I had won the Triple Crown until the next day when I read it in the newspaper. It said, "Red Sox Champs," and then it went into page two, "Yaz Wins Triple Crown." And that's the first time that I knew I had won the Triple Crown. Nobody even mentioned it to me during the season. In the last two weeks in Baltimore or somewhere like that, Frank Robinson was ahead of me in batting average by about five or six points. And Lonborg was pitching. And I can remember him coming up to me and saying, "Hey, get some hits today because I'm going to give Frank an 0-for-5." I don't know if he was referring to the Triple Crown, the batting average, the batting title, or whatever it was. But it's the only time anybody ever mentioned the Triple Crown to me, or the batting title, or anything else.

It was a magical season. I think the reason it was so magical was because we bounced back—personally, I didn't think we would—when Conigliaro got hit. He was such a big key to our team at that time. And we were just thinking, "Who's going to replace him?" I thought it was all over. I thought, "Well, there goes our chance for a pennant." Because you don't lose a player of that caliber and replace him. And just everybody else stepped up—Tartabull, Hawk Harrelson. And they did the job. Bouncing back from that, from when he was beaned to winning the pennant, I think was something even more extraordinary.

Joe Morgan

Joe Leonard Morgan
Born: September 19, 1943, in Bonham, Texas
MLB debut: September 21, 1963
Final game: September 30, 1984
Teams: Houston Colt 45s/Astros (1963–1971, 1980),
    Cincinnati Reds (1972–1979), San Francisco Giants
    (1981–1982), Philadelphia Phillies (1983), Oakland A's
    (1984)
Primary position: Second base
Bats: Left—**Throws:** Right
Hall of Fame induction: 1990
Vote: 363 votes of 444 ballots cast, 81.76%

Debuting with the Houston Colt .45s two days after his 20th birthday, Joe Morgan spent nine seasons in Houston before he was packaged in a trade to the Cincinnati Reds after the 1971 season, becoming one of the main cogs in the Big Red Machine.

He was a 10-time All-Star, including eight straight seasons, matching his tenure with the Reds. From 1973 through 1977 he was the National League's Gold Glove winner at second base. He won the first of his two consecutive National League MVP awards in 1975, batting .327, slugging .508, with a .466 on-base percentage, 17 home runs, 94 RBIs, 107 runs scored, 132 walks, and 67 stolen bases. And he led the Reds to the first of their back-to-back World Series titles that year, with a Series-winning, Game 7, ninth-inning RBI single against the Red Sox.

In 1976 Morgan followed that up with another stellar season, another MVP award, and another World Series championship, hitting .320, slugging .576, with a .444 on-base percentage, 27 home runs, 111 RBIs, 113 runs scored, 114 walks, and 60 stolen bases. The Reds went on to beat the Yankees in the World Series.

In his 22-season career, Morgan led the league in on-base percentage in 1972 (.417), 1974 (.427), 1975 (.466), and 1976 (.444); slugging percentage in 1976 (.576); runs scored in 1972 (122); triples in 1971 (11); walks in 1965 (97), 1972 (115), 1975 (132), and 1980 (93); and times on base in 1972 (282).

He retired with a .271 career average, 2,517 hits, 268 home runs, 1,133 RBIs, 1,650 runs scored, 1,865 walks, and 689 stolen bases against 162 times caught for an 81 percent success rate in 2,649 games.

Leading your team to its first World Series championship in 35 years with the Series-winning, Game 7, ninth-inning, two-out single to drive in the winning run—after being down by three runs—in the opponents' inhospitable park, after an emotional 12-inning loss in Game 6, creates an indelible memory. Some have called that 1975 World Series the greatest ever played. Others think that way only because it was their team that won.

The one that probably stands out the most for me would probably be the seventh game of the World Series in 1975. There were several other games that over the years were important, but that was the first time I won a world championship.

Game 7s are always not only emotional, just tough to relax in, tough to play your normal game. Everybody wants to do something special, not necessarily to be the hero but just to do something special and help their team win. But that's when guys try to do too much and they end up doing nothing. So I've always felt that the guys who are able to relax in the seventh game were the ones who would perform the best.

I remember standing on the line before the game and how intense everything was. But once the game started, you just start playing, and you kind of forget. You just go play the game. I don't even remember how they got three runs, I just know we were trailing 3–2 in the late part of the game. Tony Perez hit a two-run homer. And then in the seventh inning Pete Rose got a base hit to tie the score at 3–3. And I got the base hit in the ninth inning to drive in the winning run. Those are the memories. I don't remember how they got their runs or a lot of the other things that happened. But those are the big kind of moments that stand out in my mind. And then, obviously, the final out when Yastrzemski hit a fly ball to center field to Cesar Geronimo. Those are the things that stand out about that game.

It's not crystal clear, though. No, in fact, it's almost the opposite with me. It's unbelievable that I can only remember certain big moments in that game. I've watched the game on television. They show it a lot on ESPN Classic and other places, and every time I watch it, I see something that I didn't remember, or something that I didn't think about. I couldn't tell you how the 27 outs happened. I couldn't tell you a lot of the situations, and I don't know why. Maybe because I was within the moment of each pitch rather than looking at the big picture.

The thing I do remember is walking toward the plate in the ninth inning. On my way to the plate I just felt like

I was going to get a base hit at that point in the game, thinking we were going to be ahead. Actually, Pete Rose was hitting in front of me, and I was hoping he would get a walk because Ken Griffey was on second base and first base was open. Pete was a switch-hitter and they had a left-handed pitcher on the mound. But the manager came out and he decided not to walk Pete intentionally, anyway, and he ended up walking, which I was glad of, because I just wanted to be the guy up there in that situation. So that's the one thing I do remember: that it never entered my mind that I wasn't going to get a base hit. After the game, I did wonder, "What if I wouldn't have gotten a hit?" and that's when I got nervous. But I was not nervous walking to the plate, because there was not one fiber of my being that thought I wasn't going to get a base hit. But that's the "moment" thing. I got nervous afterward; what if I wouldn't have gotten a hit, and we didn't win? That's what I thought about afterward. But when I was playing I just wasn't thinking that way, not that particular time anyway.

After Game 6 my personal feelings were probably a lot different than everyone else's. I remember after the game, Pete was saying he was glad to play in the greatest game. I didn't feel that way because we lost. It's not a great game if my team loses. That's the way I felt. But I did say to the reporters, "We'll win tomorrow because we have the best players, and if I take the field with the best players, I should win." And whether it's one game or six games or whatever, if I have the best players, we should win, and I know we have the best players. I knew that we were able to perform under pressure. So I felt like we were going to win because we had the best team. That was really the way I felt. And the emotion of the sixth game, for me, was over, really. When I got back to the hotel, I started thinking about Game 7, and the fact that Bill Lee was going to pitch, what we were going to do, what I needed to do to help my team win. I left the sixth game. When I got to the ballpark for Game 7, it seemed like the sixth game was something that happened five years ago for me. It wasn't something that had happened yesterday. And there were too many things that happened in that World Series to change it anyway. So focusing on just one game was not something that I would do; I never think of negatives. We had lost the game, so then it was 3–3. It would have haunted me if we lost Game 7. But it was Game 6, so we hadn't lost anything. If you feel that you're the best team or your teammates are the best, then your confidence level should be very high; mine was, and I think our team's was. Everybody on the team knew that we were not going to blow it. We were not nervous. We knew we were going to go out there and play a good game.

Bill Lee didn't faze us. No one fazed our team. We were the Big Red Machine, the best team. I've always felt that there were very few pitchers that could ever make us feel like underdogs. There were a lot of great pitchers in our league, the Seavers and all those guys in the National League. But we never felt like they were going to beat us. We felt like our lineup was such a variety of hitters that no one pitcher could dominate all of them. We were all different hitters and we all had different strengths, and that's what made us a great team. It wasn't just that we were great players. We all brought different elements to the table and we didn't think any pitcher could handle all of those elements. We had speed. We had power. We had good hitters. We had great base runners. We had guys who could take a pitch or take a walk. We had guys who would do anything necessary to win the game. In the past, not so much today, pitchers could get in a groove against certain teams—throw a fastball, slider away to a right-hander if he's a right-handed pitcher. You couldn't pitch our right-handed hitters that way. All of them were different. Foster was different than Bench. Bench was different than Perez. Concepcion was different than Foster. Therefore, a pitcher had to make adjustments to each one in every at-bat, and that's very difficult to do. Usually, a pitcher likes to get in a groove with his fastball or his slider or whatever he's throwing. But with our team, you couldn't do that. Like Bill Lee, he chose to throw that slow curveball to Tony Perez. Now, that's probably the only guy in the lineup you couldn't throw that pitch to. He could throw it to everybody else. But he couldn't throw it to Perez. And there were guys that thought they could throw a high fastball to. Well, you couldn't. The fact that we were such different hitters is what made us such a great team.

I think it was an interesting World Series because of the personalities on both teams. The Tiants and all the great players they had, Lynn, Rice. There were a lot of guys on both teams who were excellent players who didn't make it into the Hall of Fame. But they were top-of-the-line players.

Now, I think it was the best World Series ever because we won. I think the real fallacy is that everyone thinks Carlton Fisk's home run won the World Series, because that was the high moment of the Series. But we won. I think it was a great Series, if not the best ever, because we won. But if we'd have lost and you asked me that question, I'd say no.

Jim Palmer

James Alvin Palmer
Born: October 15, 1945, in New York, New York
MLB debut: April 17, 1965
Final game: May 12, 1984
Team: Baltimore Orioles (1965–1967, 1969–1984)
Primary position: Pitcher
Bats: Right—**Throws:** Right
Hall of Fame induction: 1990
Vote: 411 votes of 444 ballots cast, 92.57%

One of the best pitchers in history and arguably the best pitcher in Orioles' history, Jim Palmer debuted as a 19-year-old and spent 19 seasons with the O's. He was an anchor on six pennant-winning teams and is the only pitcher ever to win World Series games in three decades.

Palmer retired with a record of 268–152, a .638 winning percentage, 2.86 ERA, and 2,212 strikeouts against 1,311 walks in 558 career games and 521 starts. In eight postseasons, he was 8–3 with a 2.61 ERA.

Despite injuries, Palmer won 20 or more games in eight seasons, and was one of four 20-game winners on the O's dominating 1971 staff. He was a three-time Cy Young Award winner, four-time Gold Glove winner, and six-time All-Star.

Palmer led the league in ERA in 1973 (2.40) and 1975 (2.09); wins in 1975 (23), 1976 (22), and 1977 (20); winning percentage in 1982 (.750); walks-and-hits-per-innings-pitched in 1982 (1.137); innings pitched in 1970 (305), 1976

(315), 1977 (319), and 1978 (296); starts in 1976 (40) and 1977 (39); complete games in 1977 (22); and shutouts in 1970 (5) and 1975 (10).

In his first postseason, the O's facing the Dodgers in the 1966 World Series, Palmer, at 20 years, 11 months, became the youngest pitcher to throw a complete-game shutout in a Series, besting LA's formidable Sandy Koufax 6–0 in Game 2, as the underdog O's swept the Dodgers. In 1999 he was ranked No. 64 on *The Sporting News* list of 100 Greatest Baseball Players.

Amazingly, and a point of pride to Palmer, in 558 regular season games and 3,947⅓ innings, and 17 postseason games and 124 innings, he never surrendered a grand slam. A situation he had to face in his first big-league appearance.

Babe Ruth League, Hawaii, 15 years old. I walked 18 in 10 innings. Then I went to center field and in the 12ᵗʰ hit a three-run home run, and we won 6–3. Came back on two days' rest and lost 2–0 in the final. No, I'm just throwing that out there. But yes, that actually happened.

Well, probably the most exciting thing was when my dad took me to Yankee Stadium like Billy Crystal's dad did in the movie *City Slickers*. Crystal's character talks about his greatest day ever: his first time in Yankee Stadium when he was nine or 10, and how it was before color television so he never realized how green the grass was until he walked through the tunnel. Well, when I was about nine I went to Yankee Stadium on a Tuesday night, and the Yankees were playing Cleveland. There were a couple home runs for the Yankees, and Allie Reynolds beat Mike Garcia, and the Yankees won 4–3. And, of course, I was a

Jim Palmer during 1968 spring training in Miami, Florida.

Yankees fan—I didn't know better at that point in my life! And then 10 years later I came in in relief in a game on Labor Day. One of our left-handers, Frank Bertaina, was a young left-handed pitcher, he got hit with a line drive. So there was a runner on first. He went to second on a sacrifice bunt. Horace Clarke singled. So now there's two runners on, but Tom Tresh and Mantle struck out. Then the next inning, Elston Howard struck out, Clete Boyer struck out.

[Palmer went five scoreless innings, striking out seven, to get the win.]

My Dad wasn't there; he had passed away. But it was just kind of funny, as a kid we always talk about role models and athletes and all that, first impressions, things like that. Who would ever envision when you're nine or 10 years old you go to Yankee Stadium and nine or 10 years later you're going to be pitching there? And that night, it was a rainy night, so the grass looked even greener. But when I pitched there, it was an afternoon game.

And then of course the Koufax shutout in the World Series. That was my first shutout ever. It happened to be when I was 20.

And I never threw a grand slam in almost 3,950 innings [3948] in the major leagues. And the second batter I ever faced was Tony Conigliaro with the bases loaded in relief of Robin Roberts. I was 19, Robin was 38 and he was my roommate with the Orioles. I don't remember exactly the date in April [April 17], but it was snow flurries. I brought the warm-up ball in, I was so nervous. [O's manager] Hank Bauer said, "Jim, this guy's a good high fastball hitter," which is what I threw. Then he said, "Are you nervous?" I said, "Well, I've never done this before," because I was a starting pitcher in A-ball, instructional league. I said, "Well, what do I do with this extra ball?" He said, "Well, I can take care of that. You try to take care of [the batters]." So the grand slam could have happened to the second guy I ever faced. [Tony C. was called out on strikes, Lee Thomas hit a two-RBI single, and Felix Mantilla grounded into a double play to end the inning.] But yeah, you remember those things.

There were a lot of tough batters. Rice hit a lot of home runs [nine], but he only hit, like, .218, I think. You know,

Carew probably got a lot of hits, but they were mostly singles. So you just kind of figure, well, if you're going to win seven batting titles, you're supposed to be pretty good. I think you really have to figure out who's better than you are, or as good. Then you just pitch accordingly. Clemente would have been a real tough out if I'd had to face him on a more regular basis other than World Series and All-Star Games.

The thing is, there's no substitute for experience. I found that out when I had Robin Roberts for my first roommate. I sat in the bullpen with Harvey Haddix and Stu Miller, and Sherm Lollar was the bullpen coach who'd been a terrific catcher with the White Sox and a lot of great staffs. So you ask as many questions as you can because you want to try to gain as much knowledge other than the times when you're out there.

Not giving up grand slams was a point of pride. Oh, yeah. Plus it's four runs. You don't have to be a math major to figure it out. Three-run home runs are like daggers. I don't even know how to describe a grand slam.

Rod Carew

Rodney Cline Carew
Born: October 1, 1945, in Gatun, Panama Canal Zone
MLB debut: April 11, 1967
Final game: October 5, 1985
Teams: Minnesota Twins (1967–1978), California Angels (1979–1985)
Primary position: Second base
Bats: Left—**Throws:** Right
Hall of Fame induction: 1991
Vote: 401 votes of 443 ballots cast, 90.52%

Selected the American League Rookie of the Year in 1967, batting .292 with eight home runs and 51 RBIs, Rod Carew gave a glimpse of what was to come during his 19-season career.

The 18-time All-Star hit .328 throughout his career, with 3,053 hits, 445 doubles, 112 triples, 92 home runs, 1,015 RBIs, and 353 stolen bases, including 17 steals of home, in 2,469 games.

Carew stole three bases in a game 10 times, spanning three decades. The first time he accomplished the feat, May 18, 1969, against the Tigers, he stole three bases in one inning.

In 1977 Carew was named the AL's MVP, batting .388 with 239 hits, 38 doubles, 16 triples, 14 home runs, and 100 RBIs. It was the closest any player had come to hitting .400 since Ted Williams's .406 in 1941.

Carew won seven AL batting titles and hit .300 or better in 15 consecutive seasons, from 1969 through 1983.

June 26, 1977, in his MVP season—the day he went 4-for-5 with five runs scored, six RBIs, a double, and a home run—stands out for Carew. He started the day hitting .396 and ended it at .403, as the Twins beat the White Sox, 19–12.

There's one, I don't remember exactly the date, but it was 1977, in Minnesota. I think during that year I was hitting .400. The White Sox came into town, and I was, I think, right around .400. I had four hits that day and I received seven standing ovations during the course of the game.

I went 4-for-5, and I think I drove in five or six runs. I was just hitting line drives all over the place. It was just one of those years that just seemed like the baseball just floated up there to the plate. It was just an amazing time for me. I don't know. I told the guys, "If you could feel what I'm feeling, hitting is so easy."

But I worked at it. People have always said, "Well, you had natural talent." But I took extra batting practice five days a week because I never wanted to get caught in a game where I couldn't make an adjustment and the pitchers were getting me out. So I worked on different things in extra batting practice so when I get in the game I could change a little bit and still be in a comfortable position. A lot of players can't do that because they're in one stationary stance position. But I could do a lot of different things and still be comfortable.

That's the game that jumps right out. Some people say, "Well, what about your first All-Star Game, playing

Rod Carew tips his cap to the record Twins crowd on June 26, 1977, in Bloomington, Minnesota, after his second-inning double against the Chicago White Sox put his batting average at .400.

against Willie Mays?" and all that. I say, "That was great, but this day was *the* day."

It was a nice sunny day and it was a bright day, people were just...there was just a buzz around the park. I was right around .400, it was a great crowd, and they were looking to see if I was going to keep climbing. And I didn't disappoint them. So it was just a good feeling. Everything just went right that day.

Steve Stone was the starter for the White Sox. I did okay against him [.360, 9-for-25] because he challenged me, and that's what I liked. He was around the strike zone, and you like hitting off pitchers that were around the strike zone. You don't have to chase bad pitches.

And we scored, we just jumped all over them, and they kept coming back. We ended up beating them 19–12. And everybody in the lineup was hitting. We had one guy [Glenn Adams], I think he drove in eight runs. But everybody on that day had caught the hit bug. It was just a great day for everybody.

I always tell people, of all the things I've done on the field, that was one of the most memorable things for me because any time I got a hit or did something, the people would give me a standing ovation. After like, the fourth one, I didn't want to go out, but they didn't sit down, because you don't want to show up the other team. And when I left Minnesota [in a trade to the California Angels February 3, 1979, for Ken Landreaux, Dave Engle, Paul Hartzell, and Brad Havens], I went to dinner, a banquet, and they asked, "What are you going to remember about Minnesota?" And I said those seven standing ovations that day. Because I think they saw me come in as a kid, as a young kid, and they saw me leaving as a mature person. They showed their appreciation for me.

It was hard to leave the Twins. It was hard. Mr. Griffith knew that I was going to be a free agent and he said that he couldn't afford to compensate. He said, "You should be compensated as well as the other guys." And so he said, "I want to give you opportunity to pick a couple of clubs that you would like to go to." Then that way he could get some young players back, which was, I think it was San Francisco, the Yankees were involved, and also California. I chose California because a couple of the guys, Danny Ford and Lyman Bostock, played with me and they told me what a great guy [Angels owner] Gene Autry was. So that's why I chose California. Plus, the weather was great.

Fergie Jenkins

Ferguson Arthur Jenkins
Born: December 13, 1943, in Chatham, Ontario, Canada
MLB debut: September 10, 1965
Final game: September 26, 1983
Teams: Philadelphia Phillies (1965–1966), Chicago Cubs
(1966–1973, 1982–1983), Texas Rangers (1974–1975,
1978–1981), Boston Red Sox (1976–1977)
Primary position: Pitcher
Bats: Right—**Throws:** Right
Hall of Fame induction: 1991
Vote: 334 votes of 443 ballots cast, 75.4%

The first Canadian inducted into the Hall of Fame, Ferguson
Jenkins made his major-league debut with the Phillies, but
appeared in just eight games before being traded to the Cubs,
for whom he won 20 or more games in six straight seasons.
He added a seventh 20-win season in 1974, going 25–12 with
the Rangers.

In 1971 Jenkins was selected the National League Cy
Young winner, with a record of 24–13, with a 2.77 ERA, and
30 complete games in 39 starts. That season he led the
league in wins, starts, complete games, and innings pitched,
with 325; strikeouts-to-walks ratio (7.11); and fewest walks
(1.02 per nine innings), while hitting .243 with six home runs
and 20 RBIs.

A three-time All-Star, Fergie finished in the top three in Cy
Young voting in four other seasons.

He also led the league in wins in 1974 (25); walks-per-nine-innings in 1970 (1.73), 1974 (1.23), 1975 (1.87), and 1978 (1.48); strikeouts in 1969 (273); starts in 1968 (40) and 1969 (42); complete games in 1967 (20), 1970 (24), and 1974 (29); and strikeouts-to-walks ratio in 1969 (3.85), 1970 (4.57), 1974 (5.00), and 1978 (3.83).

Upon his retirement, after 19 seasons, Jenkins had compiled a record of 284–226, with a 3.34 ERA, and 3,192 strikeouts, against just 997 walks in 664 games, 594 starts, and 267 complete games.

Although Jenkins never appeared in the postseason, moving your team into first place—after a significant absence in that position—leaves an impression.

Well, in 1967, the Cubs went into first place. They hadn't been in first place for 20-something years. And I beat Cincinnati. The Cardinals were playing the Mets. So we had to wait about 45 minutes to an hour to get the end result for them to put the W flag up. And about 30,000 to 40,000 people stayed in the stands to wait for that flag to be flown.

I pitched that game. I beat Cincinnati, [4–1]. That was kind of the start of us drawing a lot of people. We drew [almost] a million fans that year and then we started going into a million-plus with the [1968], 1969, 1970, 1971 team. Now they draw 3 million people all the time.

The Reds had some tough guys in the lineup. Pete Rose was tough. Tony Perez was tough on me from time to time. So, there were certain guys that you had to give them a lot of respect.

We had a good ballclub. It was just the fact that we were looking to get back in contention, because of the fact that the Cubs hadn't been first in the division for quite a long time. When I joined the club in 1966, we lost 103 ballgames. In 1967 they were a little better, and we were all maturing about the same time. So, in fact, we did go into first place that particular month, and I'm not sure what date it was [July 2], but we waited for the Cardinals-Mets score, and along with about 30,000 to 40,000 fans, wanted to see the "W" flag fly and to let everybody know that our flag was on top of the banner there in first place.

It was nice to see. So there were a lot of things happening, very, very good things for the Chicago Cubs.

I think because I'd gotten a lot of praise from the organization, and [manager] Leo [Durocher] kind of looked to me to try to set the stage a lot of times. I was pretty proud of that fact, and being the winning pitcher.

And it jump-started the city. People became more Cubs fans than White Sox fans. The strong teams in Chicago, they were the Bulls and the Blackhawks. So we were kind of a second team to a lot of those organizations. And when we started to win, people started to look to us to be a part of that city. I think it's really, over the years, turned into the fact that the team looks now and the city looks now for the Cubs to be a winner.

Gaylord Perry

Gaylord Jackson Perry
Born: September 15, 1938, in Williamston, North Carolina
MLB debut: April 14, 1962
Final game: September 21, 1983
Teams: San Francisco Giants (1962–1971), Cleveland Indians
    (1972–1975), Texas Rangers (1975–1977, 1980), San Diego
    Padres (1978–1979), New York Yankees (1980), Atlanta
    Braves (1981), Seattle Mariners (1982–1983), Kansas City
    Royals (1983)
Primary position: Pitcher
Bats: Right—**Throws:** Right
Hall of Fame induction: 1991
Vote: 342 votes of 443 ballots cast, 77.2%

Although best known for the infamous spitball, Gaylord Perry compiled an impressive resume in his 22 seasons: a record of 314–265, with a 3.10 ERA, 3,534 strikeouts, and 303 complete games in 690 starts.

After signing with the San Francisco Giants as an amateur free agent in 1958, Perry made his big-league debut in 1962, appearing in 13 games that season before being returned to the minors. He was back in the big leagues in 1963, working mostly out of the bullpen before joining the rotation in 1966. Perry played for eight teams in his career but was inducted into the Hall as a member of the San Francisco Giants.

He was the first pitcher to win the Cy Young Award in each league—in 1972 with the Indians, and in 1978 with the Padres.

With his seventh team, the Mariners, Perry became the 15th member of the 300-win club, beating the Yankees May 6, 1982, becoming the first pitcher to reach the milestone since Early Wynn in 1963.

In 1966 Perry won 20 of his first 22 decisions, before finishing the season at 21–8.

On September 17, 1968, he pitched a no-hitter, beating the Cardinals and Bob Gibson 1–0.

After being traded from the Giants to the Indians in November 1971, he won his first Cy Young Award in 1972, going 24–16 with a 1.92 ERA and 234 strikeouts against 82 walks, allowing 253 hits in 343 innings. Before being traded to the Rangers in June 1975, Perry compiled a record of 70–57 for the Indians—who never finished better than fourth in his time in Cleveland—accounting for 29 percent of the Tribe's victories in that time.

On his way to his second Cy Young Award in 1978 with the Padres, he reached the 3,000-strikeout mark October 1 —just the third pitcher to reach the milestone—ringing up the Dodgers' Joe Simpson in the eighth inning. Perry pitched 10 innings of the Padres' eventual 4–3, 11-inning win. He finished the season with a record of 21–6 with a 2.73 ERA, with 154 strikeouts and 66 walks in 261 innings. Among the 241 hits he allowed that season, just nine were home runs. He recorded 25 percent of the Padres' 84 wins.

Perry had a streak of 40 scoreless innings from August 28, 1967, through September 10, 1967, and 39 scoreless innings from September 1, 1970, through September 23, 1970, including four consecutive shutouts.

He led the league in wins in 1970 (23), 1972 (24), and 1978 (21); winning percentage in 1978 (.778); walks-per-nine-innings in 1981 (1.43); innings pitched in 1969 (325⅓) and 1970 (328⅔); starts in 1970 (41); complete games in

Gaylord Perry pitches to Don Clendenon in the fifth inning of a game against the Pittsburgh Pirates at Candlestick Park on June 1, 1967.

1972 (29) and 1973 (29); and shutouts in 1970 (5). He also led the league in wild pitches in 1973 (17) and 1982 (13).

Despite his long association with the spitball, Perry was ejected just once for doctoring a baseball.

A five-time All-Star, he is third all-time with 13 consecutive 15-win seasons, from 1966 through 1978, behind Greg Maddux, with 17, and Cy Young, with 15, and won 20 or more games in five seasons.

Gaylord and his brother Jim, who pitched for 17 seasons, are the second-winningest brother duo in history, with 529 combined victories, behind Hall of Famer Phil Niekro and his brother Joe, with 539.

In 1999 Perry was ranked 97th on *The Sporting News* list of 100 Greatest Baseball Players.

After that many seasons and milestones, it can be difficult to narrow memories to just one game. Nothing wrong with that.

Well, finally getting to the big leagues and staying was a great memory, because that's what you dream about doing. For one game, there was a no-hitter I had in 1968. And then going over and winning the Cy Young in Cleveland is very special, because you just got traded, you know. You didn't want to get traded, but you did. But, well, you had to survive, because Cleveland had lost 102 games the year before. So how were you going to win 20-some games? But we did it. Guys played really good when I pitched. And then winning 15 in a row in 1974 was very special. And I won a second Cy Young in San Diego in 1978. Had the great Ozzie Smith at shortstop, Winfield in right, and the great

Rollie Fingers in the bullpen. So I didn't have to pitch too many nine innings. So it was great. I've been very fortunate to have a lot. And then winning No. 300 in Seattle in 1982 was very special.

But the icing on the cake was making the Hall of Fame here in Cooperstown. Went in with two great guys, Fergie Jenkins and Rod Carew. And the most exciting thing about that, when I turned around and saw the Hall of Famers behind me. There was Ted Williams, Joe DiMaggio, Whitey Ford, Yogi, Willie Mays, McCovey, Marichal. It was so exciting. So I said, "Hey, I must have done something right." But it was great.

In my debut game, I got the first hitter out, [Don Blasingame], the second baseman for Cincinnati. He hit a [pop fly] to second base, and we got him out. I did not get a decision in that game [Giants won 13–6 in San Francisco]. I don't know whether you call it nervous. I was very excited about being there. I probably had a few nerves to it. But mostly excited.

My next game I pitched against Pittsburgh, and I got my first win. [The Giants beat the Pirates 8–3 in Pittsburgh.]

It took me about three years to get started after I got there. So it was harder to stay there than it was to get there. Well, you only get a few chances, and when you get that chance, you better be ready. And it took me a while. I got the chance, I pitched 10 innings in relief against the Mets in New York. Got the win, and they said, "Well, we are going to give you another shot." [That was May 31, 1964, at Shea Stadium, in the second game of a doubleheader, going 10 innings of a 23-inning game, allowing no runs on seven hits, one walk, striking out nine—after going two scoreless innings the day before, giving up two hits, no walks, nine strikeouts], and I didn't give it up until I retired in 1983. So, I made good use of that game.

There were so many tough batters. Billy Williams hit more home runs [nine] off me than anybody. He and Pete Rose got a lot of base hits. Mike Schmidt [9-for-24, .375], George Brett [17-for-58, .293] was very tough. I played with Orlando Cepeda and then played against him, and he was a great hitter both times, against me and for me. But I was very fortunate to play with the greatest player, Willie Mays in center for me. And then the most pure hitter I saw was in McCovey at first base. And Juan Marichal was just a great, great pitcher. So I was very fortunate.

Rollie Fingers

Roland Glen Fingers
Born: August 25, 1946, in Steubenville, Ohio
MLB debut: September 15, 1968
Final game: September 17, 1985
Teams: Oakland A's (1968–1976), San Diego Padres
(1977–1980), Milwaukee Brewers (1981–1982, 1984–1985)
Primary position: Pitcher
Bats: Right—**Throws:** Right
Hall of Fame induction: 1992
Vote: 349 votes of 430 ballots cast, 81.16%

After signing with the Kansas City A's as an amateur free agent in 1964, Rollie Fingers helped to define the closer's role throughout his 17-year career.

Known as much for his handlebar moustache, which he grew as part of the A's "Moustache Gang," as for his durability and consistency, Fingers regularly pitched multiple innings in his relief appearances.

In 1981, his first season with the Brewers, Fingers won both the AL MVP and Cy Young Award, with a record of 6–3, 28 saves, and a 1.04 ERA in 47 appearances. In 78 innings, he allowed just nine runs on 55 hits, striking out 61 while walking just 13.

In 1980 Fingers broke Hoyt Wilhelm's all-time saves record, retiring in 1985 with 341, which stood as the record until 1992, when Jeff Reardon surpassed it. He finished with a record of 114–118 and a 2.90 ERA. He pitched 1,701 innings in 944 games, 907 games out of the bullpen, finishing 709 games.

In 1974 he was named World Series MVP with two saves and a win in the A's five-game victory over the Dodgers.

A seven-time All-Star, Fingers led the league in appearances in 1974 (76), 1975 (75), and 1977 (78); saves in 1977 (35), 1978 (37), and 1981 (28); and games finished in 1975 (59) and 1977 (69).

In 1992 he became just the second reliever, with Wilhelm, inducted into the Hall of Fame. In 1999 Fingers was ranked 96th on the *The Sporting News* list of 100 Greatest Baseball Players.

He appeared in 30 postseason games, including 16 World Series games, going 2–2 with six saves and a 1.35 ERA. His A's won three consecutive World Series, beginning with the 1972 Series, when he pitched the final six outs of the seventh game against the Reds.

Probably getting the last out of the seventh game of the World Series against Cincinnati in 1972. It was nerve-wracking in that you envision yourself being on the mound for the seventh game of the World Series and getting the last out, and then all of a sudden you're there, then it's gone. It seemed like it was a 15-second thing and then it was over. It seemed like it was just 10 or 15 seconds. It went by so fast. But I got Pete Rose to fly out to left field to win the '72 World Series. So that one sticks out in my mind because that was the first World Series we won in Oakland. And that's just something that you dream about as a kid, and to be put into that situation. I came in and did a job, which is much more gratifying than not doing it.

Without a doubt, I wish I could go back and slow things down. You don't think about everything that happened during the World Series. I think back to 1972 and I can remember bits and pieces of some of the games, but not everything. I have to go back and see video to remember it all. But I look at box scores and what-not of that Series just to try and remember exactly what did happen in certain situations. But you can't remember every pitch or every play. The ones that stand out you do, but not every one. But, yeah, it goes by so fast that you don't think it's going to mean anything later on in your life. And then you start thinking about it and you think, "Dang! I wish I'd slowed down and tried to remember all this." But that's not always the way it works out.

Going into that game and that Series, well, we knew we were good because we just won the American League. We beat Detroit in 1972. We felt pretty good about ourselves. But that year we weren't supposed to win. The Cincinnati Reds, the Big Red Machine, Johnny Bench, Tony Perez, Joe Morgan, Pete Rose, you know, the whole Big Red Machine of Cincinnati was supposed to walk right over the top of us. So I think there was more pressure on them to win because they were supposed to win, than there was on us. So we just kind of went into it, saying, "Hey, we're just going to play ball." And we won the first two games in Cincinnati. Then we told ourselves, "Hey, we got a chance to win this thing." So we just started playing better.

But they were tough. They didn't have any holes in their lineup. They were strong all the way down to the eighth spot. That's why they were in the World Series.

I faced Rose two or three times [in the Series]. I know he got a base hit off me in Game 5 to beat me. But I can't remember if I faced him before that or not. I know I faced

Rollie Fingers gets drenched in champagne during victory celebrations in the dressing room after winning the World Series against Cincinnati on October 22, 1972.

him at least once in Game 5. I may have faced him in Game 3 or 4 somewhere along the line. I don't know because I pitched in six of the seven games. So where I faced him in the other games, I'm not sure [Fingers walked him in Game 1 and retired him an inning earlier on a fly ball in Game 5].

But I remember the base hit. You always remember the ones that hurt you, because that's bad. And then the final out, that's the one that counted. The other stuff I could give a you-know-what about.

Being on the mound for the last out of a World Series, it was something you dream about. But then you're in that situation and you don't think back to, "Hey, when I was a kid I thought about this." You're too wound up into the game and what you're trying to do. So you think about it later. But at the time, just being in that situation, having the opportunity to get the last out was mind-boggling for me. So after you can think about it, "You know, when I was a kid I dreamed about that." But while it's happening, it's here and it's gone. It happened so fast.

Dave Duncan, my catcher, was the first one to reach me on the mound [after that last out]. He was the first one. Sal Bando was the second. And then I think Gene Tenace was the third. And then after that, I don't know. The closest guy to you can get to you first. I remember Dave Duncan, my catcher, was first, and Sal Bando was second. After that, it was just kind of a mob scene.

I've talked to Rose about it. Oh, yeah. He had I don't know how many at-bats in the major leagues. And he had quite a bit of success, but he said if he could have one at-bat back, it would be that one. He said he probably wouldn't have swung at it. He probably would have taken it for a ball.

It was a fastball, away, up and away. It was a ball and he just swung and hit a nice little, old lazy fly ball to Joe Rudi in left field. And he always told me if he had one at-bat to take back, that would be it.

It was first pitch, fastball away. I was surprised he swung at it, to tell you the truth, because when it left my hand, I could see it was going to be away and be a ball. And then he swung at it. I was trying for a strike, but when a guy swings at a ball and hits a fly ball, you got to take it. I'm not going to say, "Hey, don't swing."

I came in in the eighth and got out of a jam in the eighth inning and then went out in the ninth inning and got the first two guys out. Then I hit a guy [Darrel Chaney]. I hit him in the foot with a breaking ball, and that brought Pete Rose up to the plate. If I would have gotten the other guy, I wouldn't even have to worry about pitching to Pete Rose.

Reggie Jackson

Reginald Martinez Jackson
Born: May 18, 1946, Wyncote, Pennsylvania
MLB debut: June 9, 1967
Final game: October 4, 1987
Teams: Kansas City A's (1967), Oakland A's (1968–1975, 1987), Baltimore Orioles (1976), New York Yankees (1977–1981), California Angels (1982–1986)
Primary position: Right field
Bats: Left—**Throws:** Left
Hall of Fame induction: 1993
Vote: 396 votes of 423 ballots cast, 93.62%

Reggie Jackson, "Mr. October," defined postseason baseball. In 27 World Series games, Reggie hit .357 with 10 home runs, 24 RBIs, slugging .755 with a .457 on-base percentage. His teams went 5–1 in six World Series, including three straight with the A's in 1972, 1973, and 1974, and two straight with the Yankees in 1977 and 1978. (He was injured in the final game of the 1972 ALCS and did not play in that World Series.) In 1973, he was named Series MVP.

A 14-time All-Star, Jackson was the 1973 American League MVP, hitting .293 with 32 home runs and 117 RBIs, slugging .531 for the A's. He finished in the top five in MVP balloting in four other seasons.

In 21 seasons, Jackson hit .262 with, 2,584 hits, 563 home runs, and 1,702 RBIs in 2,820 games.

Reggie led the league in slugging in 1969 (.608), 1973 (.531), and 1976 (.502); runs scored in 1969 (123) and 1973 (99); RBIs in 1973 (117); home runs in 1973 (32), 1975 (36), 1980 (41), and 1982 (39); extra-base hits in 1969 (86) and 1975 (78); intentional walks in 1969 (20) and 1974 (20); and at-bats-per-home-runs in 1973 (16.8), 1980 (12.5), and 1982 (13.6).

In 1999 he was ranked No. 48 on *The Sporting News* list of 100 Greatest Baseball Players.

In the Yankees' 1977 World Series win over the Dodgers, in six games Mr. October had five home runs, four in consecutive at-bats over two games (with a walk between the first and second), three on consecutive pitches in the decisive Game 6.

One favorite game, the day I hit the three homers. How could I leave that out? What else can I say? I've had a lot of good times, but my great memories are not of games. They're of my father at the Hall of Fame. Conversations with Yogi. Conversations with Mickey. Conversations with Whitey. Those are some of my great moments. Conversations with George lately. It's the memories that you share with the people that you grow to love and the people who are extremely important in your life. Those are more important than the games, really.

When I met Jackie Robinson. One night at a dinner, I introduced Rachel Robinson. Times with Willie Mays. Those are my great moments.

But the night of the three homers [during batting practice], I remember Dick Young was around the batting cage, and Dave Anderson, those guys, Steve Jacobson [sportswriters]. As I took batting practice, I hit off of Dick Howser. I hit the last five minutes. The Dodgers were sitting on the left-field line waiting to take the field. And I hit from 6:40 to 6:45. If I had 50 swings, I hit 40 balls in a 30- to 40-foot radius in right-center field and got a standing ovation when I left batting practice. And the first time up, got the walk [off Burt Hooton]. And I was praying for them to throw a strike, and next time up, I hit the first pitch for a home run. Next time up, I hit the first pitch for a home run. I was kind of glad when they brought [Elias] Sosa in [for the second home run]. And then the last time up they brought in another pitcher, a knuckleballer [Charlie Hough]. I couldn't believe it. And I hit his first pitch for a home run. I remember running around the bases. It felt like I was two or three feet off the ground. And the picture in the *Daily News* the next day, it was, "Reggie, Reggie, Reggie," and I was between shortstop and third and both feet were off the ground when I was running. And that's really how I felt. It captured my feelings at the moment. Just feeling like I was off the ground. I had a day in the life of Babe Ruth. My dad was in the stands. My mother was watching on TV. What more could you ask for? That was it for me.

Mike Schmidt

Michael Jack Schmidt
Born: September 27, 1949, in Dayton, Ohio
MLB debut: September 12, 1972
Final game: May 28, 1989
Team: Philadelphia Phillies (1972–1989)
Primary position: Third base
Bats: Right—**Throws:** Right
Hall of Fame induction: 1995
Vote: 444 votes of 460 ballots cast, 96.52%

Mike Schmidt was the embodiment of a third baseman. As powerful as he was at the plate, he was equally sure-handed in the field.

After signing with the Phillies in 1971 out of Ohio University, Schmidt made his big-league debut in 1972, with his breakout season coming in 1974, when he hit .282 and slugged .546, with 36 home runs, 116 RBIs, and 23 stolen bases, establishing a sign of what was to come over his 18-season career.

A three-time National League MVP—in 1980, 1981, and 1986—Schmidt also finished in the top 10 in MVP balloting in six other seasons. He won six Silver Sluggers, 10 Gold Gloves, and was named to 12 All-Star teams, including 1989, when he was voted in by fans after announcing his retirement earlier that season.

Schmidt led the league in slugging in 1974 (.546), 1980 (.624), 1981 (.644), 1982 (.547), and 1986 (.547); on-base percentage in 1981 (.435), 1982 (.403), and 1983 (.399); runs scored in 1981 (78); total bases in 1976 (306), 1980 (342), and 1981 (228); home runs in 1974 (36), 1975 (38), 1976 (38), 1980 (48), 1981 (31), 1983 (40), 1984 (36), and 1986 (37); RBIs in 1980 (121), 1981 (91), 1984 (106), and 1986 (119); walks in 1979 (120), 1981 (73), 1982 (107), and 1983 (128); intentional walks in 1981 (18) and 1986 (25); being hit by a pitch in 1976 (11); sacrifice flies in 1979 (9) and 1980 (13); and at-bats per home run in 1974 (15.8), 1980 (11.4), 1981 (11.4), 1983 (13.4), 1984 (14.7), and 1986 (14.9).

He led the Phillies to the postseason six times, and a World Series championship in 1980—the team's only World Series title until 2008—hitting .381, with a .714 slugging percentage, .462 on-base percentage, two home runs, and seven RBIs, being named the World Series MVP.

Mike Schmidt comes around with the bat after smacking a home run off a George Medich pitch during the eighth inning on April 21, 1976.

Upon his retirement, Schmidt had an average of .267 with a .527 slugging percentage, 548 home runs, 1,595 RBIs, and 174 stolen bases in 2,404 games. His eight home-run titles are a record in the National League, one ahead of Ralph Kiner's and second only to Babe Ruth's 12 titles. He hit 30 or more home runs in 13 of his 18 seasons, including three seasons with 40 or more.

In 1999 he was selected for Major League Baseball's All-Century Team and was ranked 28th on *The Sporting News* list of 100 Greatest Baseball Players, as the highest-ranking third baseman. *The Sporting News* had also named him its Player of the Decade for the 1980s.

Schmidt's Hall of Fame plaque in Cooperstown cites, among his other accomplishments, a game in 1976. Down 12–1 to the Cubs in Chicago, Schmidt went 5-for-6 with four home runs, four runs scored, and eight RBIs.

In 1976, April 17, I hit four home runs in a game at Wrigley Field. Let's see, who were the pitchers? I know two of the pitchers were the Reuschel brothers, Rick Reuschel, who had a pretty good career in the 1980s and 1970s, and his brother Paul, were both on the Cubs. There was a reliever, Mike Garman.

It was early in the year, about the [fifth] game of the year. I was struggling, pressing a little bit as a hitter. We were on the road, and we came from Montreal to Chicago. It was a beautiful day, a spring day in April. The breeze was blowing out a little bit. A warm day. We fell behind in the game. They pounded our starter, and we got five or six runs down. I remember my first at-bat I flew out to center field. My second at-bat I got a single to left field. My third at-bat I hit a home run.

We started to close the gap in the game as it got midway. Our bullpen held the Cubs down, and the Cubs didn't add on—well, I shouldn't say that because we ended up winning the game 18–16.

In my fourth at-bat I hit another home run. So I'm starting to feel pretty good. At that point in time, I'm 3-for-4 with three or four RBIs, whatever it was. I had a pretty good day going. And we're starting to climb back into the game, it's starting to get close now. My fifth at-bat I hit a third home run in a row, which was a pretty good achievement in itself. And we are now in the eighth or ninth inning of the game. In fact, the game went 10 innings. And we caught them. Now we've got ourselves a real ballgame.

And as it turns out I'd gotten my sixth at-bat in the game with three home runs already. I'm 4-for-5 with three home runs and I ended up I believe it was a two-run home run, I'm not sure. I can't remember that exactly. But my fourth home run won the ballgame. We won the game 18–16.

It is kind of funny. I don't remember the details of things like that. I can remember the at-bats, but not the details. I can remember home runs, but not the details. They're not quite as clear as they used to be. I can remember golf shots, though. Over the last 10 years, I can tell you about a 4 iron I hit at this course or a driver I hit over there, that 80-foot putt. I can remember those pretty vividly. But can't remember back into the baseball career.

The first really nasty pitcher for me was Tom Seaver. Well, in chronological order, it would be Bob Gibson. I faced Bob Gibson right at the end of his career, [28] at-bats. Nasty, because he was old and I didn't face him in his prime. He probably was the most intimidating pitcher of all time to anybody. People talk about Nolan Ryan. They go way back and they talk about some of the guys in the old days. But Gibson, I think to this day still holds the career mark for lowest earned-run average in a league [1.12 in 1968, fourth overall best in the modern era]. And he was automatic. Intimidating, for a young guy like me when I faced him. I watched him pitch in the World Series for years and admired him so much as a young kid growing up. Then I'm in the batter's box against the guy. Then it was Seaver, who wasn't intimidating, he just threw real hard. He was young, in his prime. He just disposed of a young kid like me pretty quick every time I'd walk up there, and that was frustrating. I didn't like facing him at all. And then in the middle to the end of my career, it was Nolan Ryan, as it is with most guys from my era. Who's the toughest pitcher, most intimidating pitcher? It would be Nolan Ryan.

That game was key in that we won 50 out of the next 68 games in 1976 and went on to be runaway winners in the National League East.

I think I was about [3-for-18] up until then, something like that. Oh, yeah, I'd say that game got me going pretty good.

Earl Weaver

Earl Sidney Weaver
Born: August 14, 1930, in St. Louis, Missouri
MLB managerial debut: July 11, 1968
Final game: October 5, 1986
Team: Baltimore Orioles (1968–1982, 1985–1986)
Primary position: Manager
Hall of Fame induction: 1996
Vote: Elected to the Hall of Fame by the Veterans Committee

Known as one of the most colorful characters in baseball, Earl Weaver was also one of the game's winningest managers, with a regular season record of 1,480–1,060, and a .583 winning percentage, 20th all-time in wins, ninth in winning percentage. In the postseason Weaver had a record of 26–20, a .565 winning percentage.

Although he had a fondness for big hits, especially three-run homers, Weaver won his managerial debut 2–0 over the Washington Senators at Memorial Stadium, as Dave McNally pitched a complete-game, six-strikeout shutout.

In his 17 seasons at the helm of the Orioles, Weaver, the "Earl of Baltimore," led his teams to six American League East titles, four AL pennants, in 1969, 1970, 1971, and 1979, and a World Series championship in 1970.

He also led the O's to five seasons with 100 or more wins— 1969 (109), 1970 (108), 1971 (101), 1979 (102), and 1980 (100)—and was named Manager of the Year three times. Just once he had a team with a winning percentage below .500, in 1986, his final season.

Well known for his colorful exchanges with the media and umpires, Weaver was ejected from 98 games, including Game 4 of the 1969 World Series, in his big-league career.

After playing second base in the St. Louis Cardinals minor-league system, Weaver began his managerial career in 1956 with the unaffiliated Knoxville Smokies in the South Atlantic League. He joined the Orioles in 1957, managing Fitzgerald in the Class D Georgia-Florida League, eventually joining the big-league team in 1968 as the first-base coach, taking over as manager in midseason.

After managing more than 4,000 games between the minors and major leagues, it may be difficult to remember just one. But with a player like Brooks Robinson on his team, April 19, 1977, at Memorial Stadium brings back fond memories—of Robinson's three-run, pinch-hit, tenth-inning, game-winning home run, his first home run of the season. It was also the 268th and final of Robinson's career.

I don't have any memories of one favorite game. My recall isn't that good. I'm sorry I don't know. I can't think of any. I mean, the whole career was better than the next. The 1970 World Series, the whole World Series watching Brooks perform was something. But there again, throughout the course of a year you got to see that often. We had some great players. And we had some pretty good pitching. Outstanding, beautiful. They were artists. McNally and Cuellar, they didn't throw the ball 90 mph. They did maybe once or twice a game. But the object was to make the opposing players hit the ball. But any one

Earl Weaver, left, meets with New York Yankees manager Ralph Houk before the start of a game at Yankee Stadium on September 15, 1972.

game? No, I don't have one. I don't remember them, to tell you the truth.

Frank scoring from third base [in Game 6 of the 1971 World Series in the bottom of the ninth on a sacrifice fly by Brooks to send it to Game 7]. But Brooks's performance, naturally winning the World Series. You know, that's stand out, but it's seven games. We did it in five. But I don't have any one particular game.

I do have one incident that stands out that I'll never forget. It was the year that, and I don't know the year, that I had to take Brooks out of the lineup. There was Bobby Grich, and I had Doug DeCinces coming through the minor leagues. Bobby had been out with an injury. I had moved DeCinces to second base so that Brooksie could get more chances. He wasn't hitting anything at the time. And when Bobby came back, I had the unpleasant job of informing Brooks that I was going to have to give the young guys a shot just to see what happens. And the young guys came through. And Brooks was part of the team then. And I called on him to pinch-hit one night in the bottom of the tenth when we were down a run. We might have been down two runs. And he hit a home run. There weren't many people left in the stands at that time, but everybody there just, it was just fantastic for Brooks to come off the bench like that. It was the left-handed pitcher LaRoche and I think it was Cleveland. But Brooksie, he was a special player. Besides when we won the World Series, seeing him get that home run, that was one of my biggest thrills. He was special.

Tommy Lasorda

Thomas Charles Lasorda
Born: September 22, 1927, in Norristown, Pennsylvania
MLB managerial debut: September 29, 1976
Final game: June 23, 1996
Team: Los Angeles Dodgers (1976–1996)
Primary position: Manager
Hall of Fame induction: 1997
Vote: Elected to the Hall of Fame by the Veterans Committee

One of baseball's most well-known figures and most popular ambassadors, Tommy Lasorda has been synonymous with the Los Angeles Dodgers for the past seven decades.

After a 14-year career in the big leagues (pitching for the Brooklyn Dodgers and Kansas City Athletics) and minors, from 1945 through 1960, with two years of military service in 1946 and 1947, Tommy worked his way through the Dodgers organization as a scout, minor-league manager, and big-league coach, eventually taking over for Walter Alston, another Hall of Fame manager, with four games left in the 1976 season.

That began a long and successful tenure for Lasorda, leading the Dodgers for 21 seasons, compiling a regular-season record of 1,599–1,439. He ranks 17th all-time in managerial wins.

Tommy led the Dodgers to eight division titles, four National League pennants (1977, 1978, 1981, and 1988), and two World Series championships (1981 and 1988).

In 1977 and 1978 he joined St. Louis's Gabby Street, who accomplished the feat in 1930 and 1931, as the only managers in National League history to win league titles in their first two seasons. He posted a record of 3–1 as the National League manager in four All-Star Games, and managed nine of the Dodgers' 16 Rookies of the Year, more than any other manager in history.

Upon his retirement as Dodgers manager in 1996, his 16 wins in 30 National League Championship Series games were a record, and his 61 postseason games as a manger were third all-time, behind Bobby Cox and Casey Stengel.

Lasorda managed the United States Olympic baseball team to a gold medal at the 2000 Summer Olympics in Sydney, Australia, just five days after his 73rd birthday, and Major League Baseball Commissioner Bud Selig appointed Lasorda as the Official Ambassador of the inaugural World Baseball Classic in 2006.

For Lasorda, the first game in his first full season of a long and celebrated managerial career is special.

———————————

O h, yeah, well I've had so many of them that it's very difficult to pinpoint just one. But I think the first game that I managed when I became the manager of the Dodgers, that was something that really was something special to me, knowing that when I went out on that field I was the manager of the Dodgers. And, you know, to get that position was not easy. There were a lot of people who they could have hired over me. But evidently, they thought I was the guy for the job. Because I had turned down about five major-league jobs because I wanted to be with the Dodgers. I wanted to manage the Dodgers. That was my goal when I started managing. I

Tommy Lasorda in 1975.

started on the bottom in the rookie league and I got to the top. When I was a player, I started at the bottom of the leagues and got to the top. So it took a lot of hard work, a lot of sacrificing, but it all came out good.

I wanted to win it, naturally, but Don Sutton pitched Opening Day, and we had to tell him that when he makes the first pitch, get the ball because it's going to go to Cooperstown for some reason. I don't know what. I don't remember. And he threw the ball, and Gary Thomasson of the Giants hit it halfway up in the bleachers on the first pitch of season. So when he came in, I said, "Hey, they were going to send the ball. They didn't want him to hit the ball to Cooperstown." So, yeah, that was the first game. But when you manage as many games as I have, it's hard to pick out what is great.

I thought Gibson's home run [in the 1988 World Series] was so much drama. There've been a lot of home runs of great importance. But they didn't have the drama attached to it that Gibson's had. He never come out for the introduction. Laying on the [trainer's] table the whole game. Then finally showed up and showed that he could hit. And that's the way it went. We couldn't put him in with less than one out. If we did, he'd be a double play easy. So I'd have to say that's a very memorable one, too.

That first game managing, there were a lot of expectations. Oh, yeah, they expect you to win. See, I was one of only two guys to win pennants in their first two seasons in the history of the National League. The other guy that did it was a guy that managed the Cardinals in 1930 by the name of Gabby Street. Imagine that though? Only two guys were able to do that, win a pennant their first two years. So that was something. And then I became only one of four who managed the same team for 20 years or more. Now, that's hard to believe. Only four guys were able to do that.

But that first game, yeah, I remember that.

Phil Niekro

Philip Henry Niekro
Born: April 1, 1939, in Blaine, Ohio
MLB debut: April 15, 1964
Final game: September 27, 1987
Teams: Milwaukee Braves (1964–1965), Atlanta Braves
(1966–1983, 1987), New York Yankees (1984–1985),
Cleveland Indians (1986–1987), Toronto Blue Jays (1987)
Primary position: Pitcher
Bats: Right—**Throws:** Right
Hall of Fame induction: 1997
Vote: 380 votes of 473 ballots cast, 80.34%

In his 24-season career Phil Niekro did as much for his signature pitch, the knuckleball, as the flutterball did for him. After signing with the Milwaukee Braves in 1958, Niekro began his big-league career as a 25-year-old with the Milwaukee Braves, finishing as a 48-year-old with the Atlanta Braves.

A five-time All-Star over three decades and a five-time Gold Glove winner, "Knucksie" compiled a record of 318–274 with a 3.35 ERA, 5,044 hits, 3,342 strikeouts, and 1,809 walks in 5,403⅔ innings over 864 games. He made 716 career starts, with 245 complete games and 45 shutouts, six of them in 1974 when he won 20 games. He had 14 consecutive seasons with 10 or more wins, interrupted by the strike-shortened season of 1981, followed by yet another five straight 10-win seasons. He had three 20-win seasons and 13 seasons of 15 or more wins.

Niekro led the league in wins in 1974 (20) and 1979 (21); ERA in 1967 (1.87); won-loss percentage in 1982 (.810); innings pitched in 1974 (302⅓), 1977 (330⅓), 1978 (334⅓); and 1979 (342); strikeouts in 1977 (262); starts in 1977 (43), 1978 (42), 1979 (44), and 1980 (38); complete games in 1974 (18), 1977 (20), 1978 (22), and 1979 (23); and he also led the league with sacrifice hits in 1968 (18).

On August 5, 1973, Niekro no-hit the San Diego Padres to go with two one-hitters and 13 two-hitters. In 1979, when he was 21–20, he was responsible for 32 percent of the Braves' 66 victories.

In 1969 he compiled a record of 23–13 with a 2.57 ERA, 21 complete games in 35 starts, four shutouts, and 193 strikeouts against 57 walks, finishing second in Cy Young Award voting to the Mets' Tom Seaver.

Phil and Joe Niekro are the winningest brother combination in baseball history, with a combined 539 wins. On June 1, 1987, with the Indians, Phil beat the Tigers 9–6, claiming the distinction for his family. At that time, Phil had 314 wins, and Joe had 216. Ironically, one of Phil's victories came against Joe, on July 4, 1967, the first time the brothers pitched against each other in a National League game. They would eventually post brotherly equitable 2–2 records against each other.

Phil bridged Braves—and baseball—pitching history, from Warren Spahn, who was 43 years old on Niekro's first major-league team, the 1964 Milwaukee Braves, to Tom Glavine, who was 21 on Niekro's final major-league team, the 1987 Atlanta Braves. His 121 wins after the age of 40 are a major-league record.

With Joe as a teammate, Phil earned his 300th win while with the Yankees on October 6, 1985, throwing a complete-game shutout against the Blue Jays, becoming the oldest pitcher, at 46, to reach that milestone with a complete-game shutout. Although the knuckleball had served him so well throughout his career, that day it was not working for him. He did not throw his signature pitch, the one his father had taught him, until the final batter of the game, a very emotional game for the Niekros. Their father was listening to the game on a phone line from a hospital bed.

My dad played for a coal-mining team back in Ohio. I got clippings of him striking out 17, 18, 19 guys a game, some really good prospects in the valley. They didn't have a lot of scouts in those days. Other guys used to tell me, "Boy, if a scout got a hold of him, he would have pitched in the big leagues." And he hurt his arm one spring. He didn't warm up going into a game, couldn't throw hard anymore. Another coal miner taught him how to throw a knuckleball to keep him pitching. And when I was old enough, six, seven, maybe eight years old, one day he threw a knuckleball to me in the backyard, and I kind of said, "What was that?" There was no spin on it. So he showed me, and then we just starting playing knuckleball in the backyard. That's all we did. See who could hit the other one in the kneecap or something like that. He did know what knuckleball pitchers were, but didn't know knuckleballs were going to get me where they got me. It was just something that when we chose teams up in the little town of Lansing, Ohio, that was the pitch I could get batters out with. And then I went out for the varsity team in high school, made it as a freshman, and pitched four years of high school ball with a knuckleball. A tryout camp came to my town, and I went there with about 200 other guys. A

Milwaukee scout evidently saw this 18-year-old kid with a pretty good knuckleball, and I signed a contract for $500 and I was off and running.

My favorite game would be, of course, my first game in the big leagues—that was getting there and being there—probably also when I was pitching in Cleveland and I beat Detroit. That made me and my brother Joe the all-time winningest brothers in baseball. We passed Gaylord and Jim Perry, and the Dean brothers. And as of now, it's still holding up, and I think it will. Not that it's a big record, but that was family pride, a family thing. That was my dad, my mother, my brother, my sister, my little town of Lansing, Ohio, all those people, my high school coaches, they were so much a big part of that. And, of course, my 300th win when I was with the Yankees.

Well, with the combined wins, I figured if I didn't get it that day, maybe Joe could get it the next. It didn't matter at all which of us got it. No, not at all. We were determined to get it. It wasn't going to make any difference in our standings because with the Indians we were pretty well out of the running in everything. But I think about my mother being there and coming on the field when we did it. It was funny because she never liked me to know she was there when the ballgame was going on. I'm going for that game, and she tells me she's not going to Cleveland, because it was about a three-hour drive. Some of her friends drove her up, and I'm thinking she's back home listening to the game on the radio, but the game starts and she's sitting right behind the catcher, about 10 rows back with a newspaper in her hand. And every time I get the sign, I see that newspaper, and I can see her little gray hair on top of the paper and her eyes sticking out the one side. And she thinks I can't see her, but I do.

Phil Niekro, here pitching in 1985, is the only knuckleballer to win 300 games.

I don't know what she was thinking, but maybe she thought she would make me nervous if I saw her sitting in the stands or something. But I didn't see anybody else but her. She was the only person I saw in the whole stands. It wasn't a big thing at the time as far as newspaper articles or reports or TV. It was just something that was very important to me and my brother Joe and my sister and my parents. There were a lot of people from my hometown. Usually when I pitched in Cleveland, that was a two and a half to three-hour drive so I was leaving a lot of tickets that year.

I was in Atlanta, and New York, and Cleveland, and Toronto. Joe started with Chicago [Cubs]. He was in San Diego, Detroit, then with us, then to Houston, New York, Minnesota. My parents didn't make a whole lot of trips. They would come down to Cleveland when we pitched. But dad worked in the coal mine. My mother's never been on an airplane. My dad flew once. So flying was out of the question, and those were long drives for them.

I spent five years in the minor leagues, one year at Fort Knox, and my big thing was I wanted to get to the big leagues and get my picture taken with a Milwaukee Braves uniform on because it was going to be in my hometown paper so everybody could see I played in the big leagues. I just wanted to be in the big leagues. Well, then I got there and I just hoped I pitched good enough to be there another day, or another week or another month, another year. And I was still pretty green at the time. So I didn't look at the long-range end of it. I didn't look at two or three years ahead. I thought, "I hope I can do well enough for this organization that they'll keep me around for another week or two or a month or a year." It was in San Francisco and I came in and got Jim Davenport out.

Before the 300th game, Joe and I stayed up all night because that was my last two-year contract with the Yankees. My father was very ill at the time and in the hospital. I won 299 games. I had five games to do that. The first two or three games after I won my 299th game, Joe and I flew back to see my dad in the hospital. And I didn't know if I was going to see him or not. That was the last game I might pitch in the big leagues, because at the time I was 46 and my contract was up with the Yankees. I didn't know if they were going to re-sign me. If they didn't, would anybody else sign me? If I didn't get it, if it was on that last day, I'd have to make a ballclub, go to spring training, and I maybe wouldn't get a chance to win it until next April. No way my dad was going to hang on that long. And Joe and I stayed up basically all night and talked about that game. And I told him, "If I get to the point where I've got this 300th game looking pretty good, I want you to come in and at least throw one pitch or get a guy out or something so when I go into the record book with my 300th win you'll be right there with me."

So we get to Toronto. It's the last game of the season, and we're two games out of first place. So that game didn't mean a whole lot other than me winning the 300th game. And all the players knew and the organization knew the situation I was in with my dad. So if I don't win this game, he is not going to hear about it. All of a sudden I'm going into the ninth inning. I've got a 8–0 lead. I get the first two guys out. The next guy [pinch-hitter Tony Fernandez] hits a double, and time out's called. I look in the dugout and Billy Martin sends Joe out to the mound, not the pitching coach, but my brother Joe. And there's 10 guys warming up in the bullpen. I'm thinking, "Boy, do you guys not think I can hold an eight-run lead?" And when Joe walked out to the mound I was going to give him my glove and say, "Here, get Jeff Burroughs out. Get him out. I know you can hold an eight-run lead with two outs in the bottom of the ninth." Then he says, "I'm not going to do that." I said, "We talked about this last night. We shook on it last night." He said, "I just found out that if you pitch a shutout, you'll be the oldest guy in the history of baseball to throw a shutout." And then he walked away from me. Then the game kind of became a little bit more important, because at that time I thought I had the 300th game pretty much wrapped up, and then I was going for the shutout.

When the game was over and everybody came out, Joe gave me a hug and told me, "I've got something to tell you about Dad." And I thought, "Oh, I don't want to know," because he was in a coma for my last four starts, and he didn't know what was going on. Me and Joe kept flying back to Pittsburgh and going down to Wheeling, West Virginia, to see him. So he really didn't hear those first four games. But that particular Sunday afternoon when I was pitching in Toronto, without me knowing it the Yankees set up a phone line, where my mother in the hospital could hear Bill White and Phil Rizzuto calling the game on the radio. She could listen to it on the telephone, and she was relaying the game to my dad, who's in a hospital bed with tubes everywhere, and they were calling the play-by-play. He hadn't said a word to my mother in three weeks. And the game was over, Joe came out to give me a hug and on the pitcher's mound he says, "I've got something to tell you about Dad." And after everybody congratulated me, he and I went and sat in the dugout. He said in the seventh inning, as my mother was relaying the game—she's a sports announcer now—to my dad, pitch by pitch, he woke up in the seventh inning and said, "Boy, Sonny's pitching a helluva game, isn't he?" He hadn't opened his eyes or said a word in four weeks, so that was what was really special about my 300th game.

Of course, me and Joe flew back the next day to see him, and he was in intensive care in a hospital room all by himself. We walked in there, and I had my Yankee hat and a ball. I signed it and told him that this 300th game was as much his as it was mine. The doctor came in and told us we had to leave. I asked why. "Why?" he says. "Well, he's been up all night waiting for you guys." I put the Yankee hat on him, gave him the ball, and I went back and pitched two more years. Joe pitched some. I got released in 1987. Joe got released in 1988, and my dad saw everything he was waiting to see. Saw one of his boys win 300, and one of his boys pitch in a World Series when Joe was with Minnesota. Two of his boys got the record. And after that we lost him.

But that was the story behind the 300th game. That was the love and the closeness. The bond that my brother and my mom and my dad and my sister had together. When I won that game, it was nice to hear what Joe told me. But it was like when I won the game that made me and Joe the all-time winningest brothers. It all came back to the backyard. Everything came back to the backyard throwing knuckleballs. My dad coming back from the coal mine and us playing catch out there, and him looking like coal miners do when they come out of the coal mine, and my mother sitting on the back porch waiting till it got dark and we'd go in and eat. We'd do the dishes. My dad would fall asleep in the living room listening to the Cleveland Indians, and get up at 4:00 or 5:00 in the morning and go back to work again in the coal mine and come home the next day. And that's all we did again. My whole baseball career goes back to that backyard. It took me a long time before I could share that with anybody, because I couldn't get through it.

The last pitch of that 300th game. They had beat us the night before for the pennant. We beat them on Friday, we're two games out. They beat us on Saturday, and that wrapped the division up for them and they were going to go to the playoffs. And I think they all were seeing double the next day because I'm sure they had their share of champagne the night before. I was just making pitches up that day. I couldn't get nobody out throwing what I did. So I went out there and just started pitching ass-backward, compared to how I always do. And then it gets down to that bottom of the ninth with two strikes on Jeff Burroughs and I called timeout. I called [catcher] Butch Wynegar out from behind the plate. He knew the situation with my dad and even before I said it, he said, "You want to throw a knuckleball, don't you?" I said, "I can't think of a better way to win my 300th game than getting the last guy with a knuckleball." And I did.

Lee MacPhail

Leland Stanford MacPhail Jr.
Born: October 25, 1917, in Nashville, Tennessee
Primary position: Executive/Pioneer
Hall of Fame induction: 1998
Vote: Elected to the Hall of Fame by the Veterans Committee

Lee MacPhail followed his father, Larry MacPhail, into baseball, and all the way into the Hall of Fame, as the two became the first—and so far, only—father-son duo to be inducted into the Hall. The MacPhail baseball bond continues as Lee's son Andy, who began his career in baseball in 1976, is currently president of baseball operations for the Orioles.

The MacPhails have won The Sporting News Executive of the Year Award three times—Larry in 1939, Lee in 1966, and Andy in 1991.

After graduating from Swarthmore College, Lee MacPhail began his 45-year career in baseball as the business manager for the Reading Brooks, before joining the Yankees, moving up through the organization as a scout, farm director, scouting director, and director of player personnel, from 1949 through 1958. One aspect of his legacy with the Yankees was the potent farm system he helped build, leading to seven World Series championships.

MacPhail joined the Orioles following the 1958 season as general manager and later became team president. Before leaving the O's in the fall of 1965 he orchestrated one of the

146

team's best trades, the acquisition of Frank Robinson from the Cincinatti Reds.

Lee returned to the Yankees as general manager in 1966 and remained there for eight years, until he was named president of the American League following the 1973 season.

During his tenure as AL president, MacPhail guided expansion into Toronto and Seattle in 1977, helped negotiate an end to the 1981 strike, and ruled that George Brett's "pine tar" home run off Goose Gossage in 1983 was legal, reversing the umpire's on-field call, ruling the game would have to be made up from that point.

In 1984 MacPhail resigned as the AL president, concluding his long baseball commitment as president of the player relations committee, representing the owners in negotiations with the players' association.

With all his accomplishments in his lengthy and successful baseball tenure, it could be hard to pick just one. But signing a switch-hitting teenager out of Commerce, Oklahoma, who would go on to be one of the game's best players is hard to forget.

I think maybe the thing that stands out most for me is signing Mickey Mantle to a contract. I was scouting for the Yankees then, and went to his home and went up to his bedroom. It was on the third floor, and I went up and signed him to a contract.

We had a scout who knew him, and he told me about him. So I'd seen him play a few games. He was about 17 years old when I first saw him. He was great. He was a very nice guy and very pleasant to be with.

I don't know exactly what caught my eye about him. He was just special. He could do everything. He was

Lee MacPhail, new president of the Baltimore Orioles, poses in front of Baltimore Memorial Stadium on December 11, 1959.

young and looked very young. He was very polite. He just seemed like a very nice person. So I was pulling for him, and I was very pleased to see him go on and have such a great career.

You couldn't expect anybody to be as good as he was. But he was special.

He enjoyed signing with us. And Tom Greenwade was there. He was our scout and the one who had really scouted him and seen him a lot. He told me all about him.

So it was fun. I thought that he was going to be a good player. I'd seen him play enough and I knew his talent was very good. Every game I saw him, he was a standout. I expected him to be a great player and he was.

I don't think there's anyone in the game today who reminds me of him. No, I don't think so. He's a tough one to duplicate.

I don't know whether it was his first game, but I remember seeing him that first year. I saw him play a lot. He was very young but had a great deal of ability. He never really looked overmatched, even when he first came up. He just fit right in. He was a natural.

There were a lot of young players that I was really fond of, but Mickey was the one.

George Brett

George Howard Brett
Born: May 15, 1953, in Glen Dale, West Virginia
MLB debut: August 2, 1973
Final game: October 3, 1993
Team: Kansas City Royals (1973–1993)
Primary position: Third base
Bats: Left—**Throws:** Right
Hall of Fame induction: 1999
Vote: 488 votes of 497 ballots cast, 98.19%

Drafted by Kansas City in the second round of the 1971 draft—one spot ahead of fellow Hall of Fame third baseman Mike Schmidt—George Brett made his big-league debut in 1973, the Royals' fifth season in existence. Brett quickly became the face of the franchise, playing his entire 21-season career in Kansas City. He was the youngest of four brothers who all played baseball, John and Bobby in the minors and Ken who was the youngest pitcher to appear in a World Series game as a 19-year-old for the Red Sox in 1967.

George also established himself as one of the best post-season performers, leading the Royals to seven postseason berths, two American League titles, and one World Series championship. In 43 total playoff games, Brett hit .337 with .627 slugging percentage, .397 on-base percentage, 10 home runs, and 23 RBIs.

In 2,707 regular-season games throughout his career, Brett hit .305, with a .487 slugging percentage, 317 home runs, 1,596 RBIs, 665 doubles, and 201 stolen bases.

A 13-time All-Star, he hit over .300 in 11 seasons and is the first player to earn batting titles in three decades, hitting .333 in 1976, .390 in 1980, and .329 in 1990.

He also led the AL in on-base percentage in 1980 (.454); slugging percentage in 1980 (.664), 1983 (.563), and 1985 (.585); at-bats in 1975 (634) and 1976 (645); hits in 1975 (195), 1976 (215), and 1979 (212); total bases in 1976 (298); doubles in 1978 (45) and 1990 (45); triples in 1975 (13), 1976 (14), and 1979 (20); extra-base hits in 1979 (85); intentional walks in 1985 (31) and 1986 (18); and at-bats per strikeout in 1976 (17.9), 1977 (23.5), and 1979 (17.9).

In 1999 George was ranked 55th on *The Sporting News* list of 100 Greatest Baseball Players.

In 1980 he was named AL MVP, making a run at the vaunted .400 mark, he reached as high as .407, going 5-for-5 on August 26, and was still at .400 with 13 games left. He finished the season at .390, with a .664 slugging percentage, 24 home runs, and 118 RBIs, and an incredible .469 average with runners in scoring position. After defeating the Yankees in the ALCS, behind Brett's three-run, seventh-inning, game- and series-winning home run off Goose Gossage in Game 3, George led the Royals to the World Series, where they fell to Schmidt and the Phillies in six games.

But Brett and the Royals would get back to the post-season in 1985, beating the St. Louis Cardinals in seven games in the World Series, when Brett hit .370.

M y favorite game would be the final game of the 1980 playoffs. That would probably rank No. 2. The No. 1 game would be the seventh game of the World Series in 1985, beating the Cardinals 11–0. Those two are the two most memorable games. Put it this way, those two games gave me the best feeling inside. Big thrills obviously to beat the Yankees after losing to them in 1976, 1977, and 1978; to finally beat them in 1980 going into our first World Series, losing in six games to the Philadelphia Phillies. But then ultimately in 1985 winning the World Series was the greatest thrill of my life.

The 1980 playoff, I remember Frank White hit a home run to give us a lead off Tommy John, and then they scratched back and took a 2–1 lead. And then I came up, and Goose was pitching, and hit a home run in the upper deck [at Yankee Stadium]. I hit a few balls in the upper deck before and since then, but that by far was probably the best swing I've ever had in my life at the most meaningful time. We were up two games to none in the playoffs. They had beat us in 1976, 1977, and 1978, and who knows what happens if you lose Game 3 because then we're playing Games 4 and 5 in Yankee Stadium. They were a good team. We were a very good team, but thank God I got that hit, because if I didn't, who knows what would have happened.

In 1985 we won Game 6 very dramatically on a controversial call at first base in the bottom of the ninth inning against the Cardinals. If we had lost Game 6, obviously there's no Game 7. And I remember going to bed about 3:00 in the morning because it was a night game, and I went out and had to get something to eat

George Brett flies in to second base as St. Louis Cardinals second baseman Tommy Herr unloads the throw to first in the first inning of Game 3 of the 1985 World Series on October 22, 1985.

and probably had to have a few beers after the game. And I remember going to bed about 3:00 and waking up at 3:05. Then I went back to sleep and woke up at 3:07. And I went back to sleep again and woke up at 3:10. And I'm thinking, "Oh, my God." And to this day I don't know if it was the adrenaline still flowing from the dramatic victory in Game 6 or being scared to death for Game 7. I didn't sleep well that night.

The Chiefs had a home game that day in Kansas City. I remember going to the Chiefs game just to get out of the house and get my mind off the upcoming game that night, a Sunday night, the seventh game of the World Series. So I went to the Chiefs game with my brother John, who came in to watch the Series. He and I went to the game, and I walked up into John Mackovic, who was the head coach of the Chiefs then. I used to sit in his suite, a lot with his wife and kids. Well, I walked up to the suite, and there's Whitey Herzog—the manager of the team we're playing, the Cardinals, is sitting in the suite, too. He knew John because Whitey still lived in Kansas City at the time. So Whitey and I are sitting next to each other. And about 2:00 in the afternoon, he says, "Come on, we got to go." So we walked from Arrowhead Stadium to Royals Stadium, which is right across the parking lot, took the elevator down together. I turned right to go in the Royals' locker room, he turned left. We shook hands, good luck, scared to death.

I remember going out and taking extra batting practice about 3:30 in the afternoon. Nobody was in the stands yet. I got somebody to come throw to me. I got some of the clubbies to go shag balls. I took about 20 minutes of good batting practice because I wanted to make sure my stroke was there, and I felt pretty good about it. John Tudor was pitching against us, who dominated us in Games 1 and 4, and he came back for a third start. And I just remember we won the game 11–0, and it was kind of a track meet. Whitey got thrown out. Joaquin Andujar got thrown out of the game. And it was just a very, very emotional time for all of us because the organization had never won a World Series before. We were down three games to one in the playoffs against the Blue Jays, three games to one in the World Series, and were able to come back in both contests. It was a great thrill to win a World Series.

People always ask me why I never became a free agent, and I always say, "Well, where was I going to go?" To me, baseball was about playing in October. Well, I came up in 1974—my first full year—and 1976 we're in the playoffs, and then 1977 and 1978. In 1979 we missed by [three] games. In 1980 we're in the playoffs, 1981 in the playoffs, 1984 we're in the playoffs. And 1985 we win the World Series. Where was I going to go? I wasn't going to go to Texas because they're never in the playoffs. I wasn't going to go to other cities, and the Royals kept giving me a five-year contract. So I'm saying, "You know, this is the best organization in baseball." We had a 10-year run, in the playoffs seven out of 10 years. To me it was the perfect place to play. Unfortunately, since 1985 we haven't sniffed anything, and I played eight more years after that. So it was a tough last eight years of my career. But, still, I was able to finish it in the town I started in, which you don't see very much anymore.

Orlando Cepeda

Orlando Manuel Cepeda (Pennes)
Born: September 17, 1937, in Ponce, Puerto Rico
MLB debut: April 15, 1958
Final game: September 19, 1974
Teams: San Francisco Giants (1958–1966), St. Louis Cardinals
   (1966–1968), Atlanta Braves (1969–1972), Oakland A's
   (1972), Boston Red Sox (1973), Kansas City Royals (1974)
Primary position: First base
Bats: Right—**Throws:** Right
Hall of Fame induction: 1999
Vote: Elected to the Hall of Fame by the Veterans Committee

After signing with the New York Giants in 1955, Orlando
Cepeda debuted with the San Francisco Giants in 1958,
hitting .312 with 25 home runs and 96 RBIs in 148 games on
his way to being unanimously selected the National League
Rookie of the Year.

   In his 17-season career, Cepeda, an 11-time All-Star
(including two games each from 1959 through 1962), hit over
.300 in nine seasons, more than 30 home runs five times, and
20 or more home runs 12 times. "Cha-Cha" or "Baby Bull" (in
reference to his father, Pedro, a well-known baseball player in
Puerto Rico), hit .297 with 379 home runs and 1,365 RBIs in
2,124 games. He also had five seasons of 100 or more RBIs
and three seasons with 100 or more runs scored.

   Cepeda was the unanimous selection for NL MVP in 1967
with St. Louis, hitting .325 with 25 home runs and 111 RBIs,

Orlando Cepeda, named 1958 National League Rookie of the Year, grins as he holds the plaque presented to him by Bob Stevens, president of the San Francisco chapter of the Baseball Writers Association of America.

helping the Cardinals to a World Series championship over the Red Sox.

Although his legacy was marred by a conviction in 1975 for drug smuggling, for which he served 10 months in federal prison, and again in a 2007 arrest in California, to which he pleaded no contest to a misdemeanor marijuana charge, Cepeda was elected to the Hall of Fame in 1999, the sixth Hispanic player elected to the Hall.

Cepeda made his big-league debut in the game in which Major League Baseball made its debut on the West Coast. The Giants beat the Dodgers, 8–0, in the first game ever played in California. Cepeda hit a solo home run for his first hit, off the Dodgers' Don Bessent, who had entered in relief of Don Drysdale.

My first big-league game, it was a dream come true. As a kid, first you want to be a ballplayer. Then you want to play in the big leagues. So my first game was my dream come true. I was nervous before the game, but once the game started, it was gone. Don Drysdale was the first pitcher I faced. Not an easy way to start—tough guy, yeah.

I did so-so against Don Drysdale. A good pitcher, tough, mean, knock you down, hit you, everything.

My first hit was a home run. The [third] time I batted, I hit a home run to right field. It was in San Francisco. It was a great day, a wonderful day. The game was great, being there was incredible. It's very easy to think back to that game. I think about it every day, because, like I say, it was a dream come true, playing a big-league game, Opening Day. It was incredible.

Willie Mays, he helped me a lot. He really helped me. He just said to do the best you can and let your ability work for you. So that's what I tried to do.

Nolan Ryan

Lynn Nolan Ryan Jr.
Born: January 31, 1947, in Refugio, Texas
MLB debut: September 11, 1966
Final game: September 22, 1993
Teams: New York Mets (1966, 1968–1971), California Angels
    (1972–1979), Houston Astros (1980–1988), Texas Rangers
    (1989–1993)
Primary position: Pitcher
Bats: Right—**Throws:** Right
Hall of Fame induction: 1999
Vote: 491 votes of 497 ballots cast, 98.8%

After being drafted by the Mets in the 12th round of the 1965 draft (the only player from that round to make it to the big leagues) out of Alvin (Texas) High School, Nolan Ryan went on to a record-setting 27-season career and was inducted into the Hall of Fame with the second-highest vote percentage in history, behind Tom Seaver's 98.84 percent.

After the 1971 season, the Mets traded Ryan, Frank Estrada, Don Rose, and Leroy Stanton to the California Angels for Jim Fregosi, the only time in his career Nolan was traded, later joining the Astros and then the Rangers as a free agent.

In February 2008 Ryan was appointed president of the Texas Rangers, the first Hall of Famer to be named president of a major-league team since Christy Mathewson served in that role for the Boston Braves in 1925.

Ryan threw a record seven no-hitters for three teams in three separate decades, recording the gems with the Angels twice in 1973, once in 1974 and 1975, with the Astros in 1981, and with the Rangers in 1990 and 1991. He was the oldest pitcher to throw a no-hitter in his last two no-no's, June 11, 1990, in Oakland, and May 1, 1991, against the Blue Jays. He also threw a record 12 one-hitters, tied with Bob Feller, and 18 two-hitters. He is the only player in major-league history (other than Jackie Robinson) to have his number retired by three teams—the Angels, Astros, and Rangers.

He debuted as one of the youngest players in baseball, and in his final season of 1993 was the oldest. Upon his retirement, Ryan had compiled a record of 324–292, with 61 shutouts, 222 complete games, and 5,714 strikeouts, over 5,387 innings in 807 games (773 starts). The all-time leader in strikeouts, he led the league in Ks in 11 seasons, and had more than 300 strikeouts in six seasons, while striking out 1,176 different batters. He is also the all-time leader in walks, with 2,795, and wild pitches, with 277.

Ryan averaged 9.55 strikeouts per nine innings over his career, and recorded 10 or more Ks in a game a record 215 times while striking out the side 331 times.

An eight-time All-Star, in 1999 Ryan was ranked No. 41 on *The Sporting News* list of 100 Greatest Baseball Players, while Major League Baseball named him to its All-Century Team.

Ryan threw each of his seven no-hitters to a different catcher. With the no-hitter, a coveted and precious accomplishment for any pitcher, holding the record for most no-nos in history is certainly memorable, including the second in a lengthy career, against the Detroit Tigers on July 15, 1973, when he had 17 strikeouts in the game, and the final, against the Blue Jays, 18 years later.

Iguess because of the length of my career and some really neat things that happened to me, there would have to be about two or three games that kind of fall into that category of being my favorite or most memorable. It would probably either be the no-hitter in Detroit—because in that no-hitter was the best stuff that I had in a no-hitter and probably from that standpoint it was a more dominating performance on my part—or the seventh no-hitter, because it happened so late in my career and it happened here in Arlington in front of the hometown crowd. That kind of stuff made it very memorable. And the fans, one of the interesting aspects of that was that there were more fans in the stands at the end of the game than there were in the first couple of innings because local people who were listening to the game got in their cars and came on over to the ballpark.

In the game against the Tigers, I remember telling Tom Morgan, the pitching coach, "Well, Tom, if I ever were to throw another no-hitter, it might be today," because that was the kind of stuff I had warming up, and it was just one of those days that everything came together.

In the last no-hitter, I did not have that feeling. No, not at all, not at all. That late in my career, those good feelings were pretty much gone.

What you would do is if you had somebody who caught you on a regular basis, then you didn't shake them off a lot because they pretty well knew how you liked to pitch and they knew the hitters and stuff. But a good example of that was John Russell, who is now the manager for Pittsburgh. The sixth no-hitter was the first time he had ever caught me. So he would just initiate pitches. But then, as the game went on, we fell into a pattern where I wasn't shaking him off much at all.

But obviously, for him like that or the first time Pudge ever caught me when he came up, his [second] big-league start was catching me. So getting thrown in a game situation like that, there's some uncertainty mainly when they enter, if they caught you in spring training or down in the bullpen or anything like that, and getting comfortable.

The only time that I had a catcher for any length of time on a regular basis was Alan Ashby with the Astros. [Ashby caught the fifth no-hitter, against the Dodgers in 1981.] So then you develop a comfort level with a catcher that catches you on a regular basis, and the way he sets up and he knows the way you want him to set up, and calling pitches, giving you a feel for how things flow.

Well, you know what, the interesting thing about the 17 strikeouts against the Tigers was I think I had 16 after seven innings and then we had a long eighth inning. When I went back out there in the bottom of the eighth, my stuff wasn't as good as it had been in the previous seven.

I think what you can do is go back to every no-hitter I threw and look at it, and the difference between it being a one-hitter and a no-hitter is a good defensive play that one of your teammates made in the game. And in that second no-hitter, Rudy Meoli caught a little soft liner out in left field. He was the shortstop. And I don't remember who hit it now, but you know that's one of those balls that when it's hit, you don't know if it's going to drop or not because you don't know if it's going to have enough carry on it. But the shortstop is going to be able to make the play because in a normal situation your left fielder can't come in that far and catch a ball like that.

Nolan Ryan is congratulated by Angels manager Bobby Winkles after throwing his second no-hitter, against the Tigers on July 15, 1973.

I'm sure my teammates probably were a little nervous. But I don't remember it because they kind of avoid you as it gets later in the game. As the game goes on, those things happen.

I've been in enough of them. I think I threw 12 one-hitters, and a couple of them were given up in the ninth inning. So I'd been there before. So I knew that until you get the last out, you hadn't done it.

I think they all are special and they all have special meanings to me. It would be hard to say if I had to pick one over the others. I don't think that I really could. The first one I threw, they all come as a surprise to you because it's not something you ever anticipate. And it's not something you can prepare for. So when it happens, I call it just one of those magical days where everything comes together.

Some of the memories are more vivid than the others. To give you an example, in Detroit the ball that Rudy Meoli caught, and then the last out of the game. Norm Cash came up to the plate with a table leg that he had screwed off a table in the clubhouse and was using it for a bat. Those kind of things. Knowing that Gates Brown was the designated hitter. I believe it was the ninth inning, but I may be wrong on that, either the eighth or ninth. I really believe it was the ninth inning. He was hitting, and I knew I didn't have as good of stuff as I had earlier in the game, and he was always a good fastball hitter. So I remember having that concern, but he hit a line drive out to the shortstop, for the second out, and that brought up Norm Cash.

Well, Cash, he went up to the clubhouse and unscrewed a table leg off the table and came up. He was the last out of the game. He walks up there, and I see he has something, but I was so wrapped up in the game that I should have just let him go ahead and hit with it. But I walked up and told [home plate umpire] Ron Luciano, "He can't hit with that." He said, "What are you talking about?" I said, "Check his bat." And Ron looked at it and says, "You can't hit with that." And Cash says, "What difference does it make? I can't hit him anyway!"

Oh, I laughed, but I knew Norm. He was a friend of mine. So that was just him. He was one of the true characters of the game at the time. And then he popped out to shortstop to end the game.

Robin Yount

Robin R. Yount
Born: September 16, 1955, in Danville, Illinois
MLB debut: April 5, 1974
Final game: October 3, 1993
Team: Milwaukee Brewers (1974–1993)
Primary position: Shortstop
Bats: Right—**Throws:** Right
Hall of Fame induction: 1999
Vote: 385 votes of 497 ballots cast, 77.5%

Drafted by the Brewers with the third overall pick in the 1973 draft, Robin Yount was the youngest player in baseball as a rookie in 1974 and was still the youngest player in the American League the following season. He was 37 when he retired 20 seasons later, with a .285 average, 3,142 hits, 583 doubles, 126 triples, 251 home runs, 1,406 RBIs, and 1,632 runs scored in 2,856 games, spending his entire career with the Brewers. He also had a combined .972 fielding percentage, including .964 at shortstop and .992 in center field, his primary positions.

In 1982 Yount won his first AL MVP award as a shortstop hitting .331 with 29 home runs and 114 RBIs. In 1989 he again was named AL MVP, this time as a center fielder, hitting .318 with 21 home runs and 103 RBIs. Robin is one of just four players, along with Hank Greenberg, Stan Musial, and Alex Rodriguez, to win the MVP Award at two different positions.

A three-time All-Star, Yount led the league in slugging percentage in 1982 (.578); games played in 1976 (161) and 1988 (162); hits in 1982 (210); total bases in 1982 (367); doubles in 1980 (49) and 1982 (46); triples in 1983 (10) and 1988 (11); and extra-base hits in 1980 (82) and 1982 (87).

In three postseason series, Yount hit .344, including the 1982 World Series, when the Brewers lost to the Cardinals in seven games despite Yount's .414 average, .621 slugging percentage, .452 on-base percentage, one home run, three doubles, and six RBIs.

To get to that postseason, the Brewers had to face the Orioles in the last game of the season with identical 94–67 records, and first place in the AL East on the line. Yount went 3-for-4 with two RBIs, four runs scored. He reached base with home runs in his first two at-bats, a triple in the eighth, and was hit by a pitch in the ninth.

The one game that stands out the most in my mind would be the last game of the season in 1982 in Baltimore where, after 161 games, the Brewers and the Orioles were tied, dead even. Last game of the season, playing each other for all the marbles in Baltimore and, personally, it was probably the best game of my career in a big situation. And we won [10–2]. So that game would be the single most exciting game for me.

I hit a couple of home runs off of [Orioles Hall of Famer Jim Palmer]. He had plenty of success on his side, too, just not that day. He did okay for himself. But for me personally that was probably the highlight.

And that year, after that one, we had four more of those win-or-go-home games shortly after because we ended up losing the first two games to the Angels in a best-of-five series. So that meant we had three do-or-die games in a row after that. We won all three of those and then went to a seventh game of the World Series. So in about a two-week span we had five win-or-go-home games. We won four of them, and unfortunately, the one we didn't win was the last one, the seventh game to win the World Series. But you know, four out of five do-or-die games, that's not too bad. Needless to say, it was an exciting year.

That was the most exciting game I ever played. Fortunately, I had a good game. It got us into the playoffs. *I* didn't get us in, but *we* got in. It was the biggest game of my career to that point. We went through the playoffs, got in the World Series. So that single game was probably the biggest leading up to getting into the playoffs. I had two home runs and a triple. So, yeah, it was the biggest game of my life at that time, and I had a big game. So that's why it was a special game for me. We scored a bunch of runs. It was just a big deal because we were trying to blow it. We had had a three-game lead, and they beat us three in a row to get even in the last game. And then to come out, I think I hit a home run in the first inning and we had a lead, and then I hit a home run the next time up. So it was the most satisfying moment, where it was do or die and we came up big. So that was exciting for us.

If we didn't win that game, we were going home. And then we had to go all the way to Anaheim and play the Angels. So we went from the East Coast to the West Coast. Believe it or not, that series was so emotional, and I think emotionally draining. It's the first round of the playoffs with a bunch of guys that hadn't been in the playoffs very often, only the year before against the Yankees was the only playoff experience the Brewers had. And I think that series against Baltimore took so much out of us, we came out to Anaheim flat. We lost the first two games in a best-of-five. We went to Milwaukee and swept them three straight to get into the World Series. So we went to the limit. Obviously the game in Baltimore was do or die, then we lost the first two to Anaheim, the next three are do or die, then we go to Game 7 in the World Series, so we had five do-or-die games in a two-week span, we won four of the five.

Unfortunately, the fifth game was the seventh game of the World Series. So we came up one game short. But it was a great year, a great thrill. If you could change the outcome of the World Series so we were the champs, it would be wonderful. But even though we came up short, it was still the highlight of my 20-year career playing in that stretch.

It's tough to believe it was that long ago. I don't like to think about it that way, because it feels like where did our careers go? It doesn't seem all that long ago we were just getting started in all of this. And now we've been done for quite a while. So that's a word to the wise: enjoy your time because it goes by awful fast. The older you get, the faster it goes by. I can promise you that. You'll find out. The older you get, the faster it goes.

Sparky Anderson

George Lee Anderson
Born: February 22, 1934, in Bridgewater, South Dakota
MLB managerial debut: April 6, 1970
Final game: October 1, 1995
Teams: Cincinnati Reds (1970–1978), Detroit Tigers
   (1979–1995)
Primary position: Manager
Hall of Fame induction: 2000
Vote: Elected to the Hall of Fame by the Veterans Committee

A light-hitting second baseman in one season with the Phillies, Sparky Anderson found his place at the helm rather than on the field, leaving his mark on baseball as one of the most successful managers in history.

Anderson took over the Reds in 1970, the youngest manager in baseball at 36, his first big-league managerial position after leading several minor-league teams and serving as coach for the expansion San Diego Padres. He retired after 26 seasons as one of the winningest managers.

In his first managerial season, Sparky guided the 1970 Reds to a record of 102–60, a .630 winning percentage, and the World Series, where the Reds fell in five games to the Orioles.

In nine seasons with the Reds, from 1970 through 1978, Anderson led the Big Red Machine to a combined record of 863–586, a .596 winning percentage, five National League

West division titles, four pennants, and two World Series championships. The 1975 and 1976 World Series champions posted a combined record of 210–114, a .648 winning percentage, the first National League team since the 1921 and 1922 Giants to win back-to-back World Series titles.

With the Reds, he finished lower than second in the NL West just once, when the 1971 team could muster a record of just 79–83, for fifth place. Sparky is the Reds all-time leader in wins, with 863, and winning percentage, at .596.

Taking over the Detroit Tigers in 1979, he is the team's all-time leader in seasons (17), games (2,580), and wins (1,331), with a cumulative record of 1,331–1,248, for a .516 winning percentage.

Sparky was the first manager to win World Series championships in each league, leading the Reds in 1975 and 1976 from the National League, and the Tigers in 1984 from the American League. His teams won more than 100 games four times, making him the first manager to reach that mark in each league.

He is the only manager to earn Manager of the Year honors twice in each league, earning the award in the National League in 1972 and 1975 and in the American League in 1984 and 1987.

A five-time All-Star Game manager, Anderson led his teams to three World Series, seven division titles, and five pennants, with a .619 postseason winning percentage. Dubbed "Captain Hook," for his penchant for going to his bullpen, Anderson was on the vanguard of current bullpen management.

He is the first manager to collect more than 600 wins in each league. Upon retiring, Sparky had the third highest win total in history, at 2,194, behind just Connie Mack and John McGraw. In 26 seasons, Anderson managed 4,030 games for a record of 2,194–1,834 and a .545 winning percentage, just the sixth manager in history to reach the 4,000-game mark, with Mack, McGraw, Bucky Harris, Tony LaRussa, and Bobby Cox.

But without that first game, the other 4,029 would not have been possible.

———

M y favorite game I ever had was the first game I managed. I was 36 years old, the youngest manager in both leagues, in 1970. I managed Cincinnati. That was my first game, and we won it. And that was probably, all my whole career, the most thrilling game I ever was in.

It was just tremendous. Always remember: there's only one first and it's always special. There's no second, just first. Second doesn't matter. Somebody told me once, "Well, somebody once tied you." No, they didn't. There's no tie. There's first, and then there's everything else.

I remember that game. It was drizzly the whole day, and it was so cold in Cincinnati that you can't believe! And Lee May hit the ball against that hard wind with the rain coming down, and he hit it right out of there. I said, "I've got a good team here." And in that same inning, Bernie Carbo homered, and Bobby Tolan homered, too. We ended up winning, I think it was 5–1.

I always try to tell people that whatever you do first will always be the best, and that was my first game, in 1970. Nothing compares to it. I was only 36 years old then. I got a little old since then, I guess.

We played the Montreal Expos that game, and Gene Mauch was managing. And Gene, he's one of my all-time favorites. And I'll never forget, we were standing there before the game, and he grabbed a hold of the side of my pants to get my attention and said, "Never forget this moment. Never forget it. It'll never happen again." And he was right. That was quite a day for me. I've always told first-time managers, "Young man, don't ever forget this moment."

Was I nervous? Oh, my God! I was nervous every game I managed, and there were over 4,000 of them! Somebody said to Earl Weaver, "When do you get nervous?" and he said, "When they throw the first pitch." But if you're not nervous, don't go there. But it was a good time, too. But yeah, I guess I was probably more nervous because it was my first game. Yeah, because that meant so much.

When they hired me, I thought that they were nuts. How can you hire someone who had never managed in the major leagues, and had only coached one year, and that was with San Diego, an expansion team in their first year? So I thought somebody around here's nuts!

But I'm going to tell you something, and this is what I believed. I never, ever was afraid to go into the river. The river is where no cowards go, and the bank, right, is for the cowards. But it's a funny thing, and I don't really know how to explain it, I never was scared. I managed 26 years in the major leagues and I never had a day that I personally was scared. I don't know why. I cannot explain it. I have no idea.

But you know something? I don't watch any games. And there is a reason I won't watch any inning of the playoffs or the World Series, is that I want to get back there when I watch it. And then I get anxious, and I don't want to get anxious. That's over and past. I had my time. And it was wonderful. In some ways it went by so fast, and in some ways no, because I know so many people and I run into so many people even though I won't go to a game, which I don't, and I won't watch a game. But still they call me a lot. I get so many calls from guys. It keeps you in it. And that's the best.

Carlton Fisk

Carlton Ernest Fisk
Born: December 26, 1947, in Bellows Falls, Vermont
MLB debut: September 18, 1969
Final game: June 22, 1993
Teams: Boston Red Sox (1969, 1971–1980), Chicago White
    Sox (1981–1993)
Primary position: Catcher
Bats: Right—**Throws:** Right
Hall of Fame induction: 2000
Vote: 397 votes of 499 ballots cast, 79.56%

A true New Englander, Carlton Fisk was born in Vermont, grew up in New Hampshire, attended the University of New Hampshire before being drafted by the Boston Red Sox with their first pick in 1967, made his big-league debut with the Red Sox in 1969 and played 10 more seasons in Boston before exchanging Red Sox for White Sox. He played another 13 seasons in Chicago, before being inducted into the Hall of Fame wearing a Red Sox cap.

In 1972 "Pudge" became the first unanimous selection as American League Rookie of the Year, hitting .293 with 22 home runs and 61 RBIs, tying for the league lead with nine triples—the last time a catcher has led in three-base hits—and also winning the Gold Glove.

Known for his work ethic and respect for the game, Fisk set a record with 2,226 games behind the plate over his 24 seasons. He also set the record for home runs hit by a catcher, with 351, since passed by Mike Piazza.

Upon his retirement in 1998, after playing in parts of four decades, Fisk had compiled a .269 average, with a .341 on-base percentage, .457 slugging percentage, 376 home runs, 1,330 RBIs, and 421 doubles in 2,499 games. An 11-time All-Star, his single in the 1991 Midsummer Classic at the age of 43 made him the oldest player to record a hit in an All-Star Game, while his 72 home runs after the age of 40 are second all-time.

Fisk gave the sport one of its most memorable moments with his twelfth-inning home run in Game 6 of the 1975 World Series, willing the ball fair, waving his arms as he hopped down the first-base line, the ball clanging off Fenway Park's left-field foul pole, forcing a decisive Game 7. The Red Sox would eventually dub the left-field foul pole the "Fisk Pole," complementing the Pesky Pole in right field. With nearly a quarter century of games to choose from, it may be difficult to pick one game that stands out among the others. For baseball fans, it's not as difficult.

––––––––––

Oh, man, it'd be pretty hard to boil down to one. I played a long time and played a lot of games. Growing up in New Hampshire, maybe my favorite time was wearing a Red Sox uniform. There's so many moments that, as I look back, jump out. But as far as one being a favorite, I don't know if I have a particular favorite game. Some favorite moments, obviously. There's one in particular. Game 6 in 1975? Ah, yeah. But there are a lot of favorite moments, too, depending on the time of the season, the

Carlton Fisk reacts as he sees his twelfth-inning home run hit the left foul pole to win Game 6 of the World Series against Cincinnati on October 21, 1975, at Fenway Park.

time of the game, and even your teammates that you played with. Some of my favorite moments wouldn't be offensive moments, anyway. It would be the way that I think I helped my pitching staff out. That was where my favorite part was, anyway.

Catching Luis Tiant was probably one of my favorite memories of all time. He was fun to catch. Talk about accountability, he was a guy that made no excuses, no blame, just he was pitching and accepted what came along. He was probably the funniest guy that ever wore a Red Sox uniform. But in that same breath, he was a ferocious competitor. So he took the game very, very seriously. He just didn't take himself overly seriously.

Game 6 [October 21, 1975], I just remember what a great game that was. And the great part about it is that every year, everybody remembers, World Series time. It's good for me, and hopefully good for the game, too.

I remember standing in the on-deck circle with Fred Lynn, and I said, "Fred, I think I'm going to hit one off the wall. So drive me in." But I hit one off the pole, and it ended the game. The rest is history. But we were ready to go home. We were tired.

I don't remember running around the bases. I remember standing there saying, "Boy, I hit that ball good," and then, "Oh, stay fair!" But I hardly remember going around the bases.

Tony Perez

Atanasio Perez (Rigal)
Born: May 14, 1942, in Ciego de Avila, Cuba
MLB debut: July 26, 1964
Final game: October 5, 1986
Teams: Cincinnati Reds (1964–1976, 1984–1986), Montreal
　　Expos (1977–1979), Boston Red Sox (1980–1982),
　　Philadelphia Phillies (1983)
Primary position: First base
Bats: Right—**Throws:** Right
Hall of Fame induction: 2000
Vote: 385 votes of 499 ballots cast, 77.15%

Signed by the Cincinnati Reds as an amateur free agent in 1960, Tony Perez became a vital part of the Big Red Machine, leading the Reds to five division titles, four National League pennants, and back-to-back World Series championships in 1975 and 1976. Perez also helped the Phillies to the 1983 NL pennant.

In his 23-season career, Perez hit .279 with 379 home runs and 1,652 RBIs in 2,777 games. He hit 90 or more RBIs in 11 consecutive seasons, and more than 100 RBIs in seven seasons. From 1967 through 1976, Perez led all major leaguers with 1,028 RBIs.

After playing third base early in his career, Perez found a home at first base, where he had a career fielding percentage of .992 in 1,778 games.

Johnny Bench (No. 5) gives Tony Perez a hand clasp after Perez hit a homer to help the Cincinnati Reds win the World Series 4–3 against the Boston Red Sox in Boston on October 23, 1975.

A seven-time All-Star, Perez was named MVP of the Midsummer Classic in 1967 in his first All-Star Game, hitting the game-winning home run in the fifteenth inning.

In 1970 Perez finished third in NL MVP balloting—behind future Hall of Famers, teammate Johnny Bench and the Cubs' Billy Williams—hitting .317, with a .401 on-base percentage, .589 slugging percentage, 40 home runs, and 129 RBIs. Perez finished in the top 10 in MVP balloting in three other seasons.

The first Cuban-born player elected to the Hall of Fame, he became the oldest player—one day before his 43rd birthday—to ever hit a grand slam, surpassing Cap Anson, who was 42 years, three months when he accomplished the feat in 1894.

Perez hit three home runs in the 1975 World Series against the Red Sox, including a sixth-inning, two-run shot in Game 7, cutting the Reds' deficit to 3–2, on their way to a 4–3 win.

I have a lot of good memories. When I played for the Red Sox—I played for the Red Sox for three years—coming in to play the Yankees was something really special, and all the series for the players, for the Red Sox, was important. But the best game was the seventh game of the World Series [against Boston in 1975]. I hit a home run, we got back in the game, and then we're winning and then it was the ninth inning. That was my best.

I remember everything about that at-bat. I remember everybody. Bill Lee was pitching. He threw me that bloop pitch, and I hit it. He threw it to me before and bounced it. I swing at it and I was embarrassed because, you know, a lot of people were there. But that was, I got it in the back of my mind that he was going to throw it, and he did, and I hit a home run.

On a pitch like that, you have to generate the power. Yes, you got to get way out on it and hit it. That was a big hit for us because we were losing 3–0 at the time.

I told Sparky, the manager, because he was worrying about it. It was the sixth inning, and we were down 3–0 and we lost that sixth game when Carlton Fisk hit that home run. He was worrying, but I told him, "Sparky, don't worry about it because if I get men on base, I am going to hit one." He just said, "Okay, okay." And then it happened. That was a big hit.

The sixth game was very important for the Red Sox. We almost won it, but they came back and tied the game and then won it. We were never down. We knew we had another game to play, and we were very, very positive. We knew we were going to win it, and we did.

Bill Mazeroski

William Stanley Mazeroski
Born: September 5, 1936, in Wheeling, West Virginia
MLB debut: July 7, 1956
Final game: October 4, 1972
Team: Pittsburgh Pirates (1956–1972)
Primary position: Second base
Bats: Right—**Throws:** Right
Hall of Fame induction: 2001
Vote: Elected to the Hall of Fame by the Veterans Committee

Signed by the Pittsburgh Pirates as a 17-year-old shortstop in 1954, Bill Mazeroski made his major-league debut two years later at second base and quickly established himself as one of the best in baseball at that position. In 2,094 games at second in his 17-season career, Maz compiled a .983 fielding percentage, above the league average of .976, along with 10 flawless games at third base.

A seven-time National League All-Star, Mazeroski earned eight Gold Gloves throughout his career, including five consecutive from 1963 through 1967. He led the NL in assists nine times and double plays eight times—major-league records for a second baseman. He also holds the record for most double plays in a season, with 161 in 1966, and has more career double plays (1,706), than any other second baseman. In 1966 he played all 162 games, and committed just eight errors, for a .992 fielding percentage, compared to the league's average of .978. He also played all of the Pirates' 163 games in 1967 and 162 in 1964.

In 2,163 games, Maz had 2,016 hits, with a .260 career average, 138 home runs, and 853 RBIs. From 1957 through 1968, he drove in more runs, 756, than any other middle infielder.

In 1960 he was named *The Sporting News* Major League Player of the Year and earned the Babe Ruth Award as the World Series MVP. In four postseasons, Maz hit .323 with a .581 slugging percentage. He was part of two World Series champions with the Pirates, in 1960 and 1971. In the 1960 World Series against the Yankees he hit .320 with two doubles, two home runs, and five RBIs. His first home run in that Series was a two-run shot in the Pirates' 6–4 Game 1 win. His next home run, leading off the ninth inning of Game 7, gave baseball one of its signature historical moments—the first walk-off, Series-ending home run in history.

I have probably two games that come to mind. The one against the Yankees, of course, in 1960, and one of my favorite games I ever played was the Harvey Haddix 12-inning perfect game. [Haddix had a perfect game through 12 innings against the Braves in Milwaukee on May 26, 1959. The Pirates had 12 hits but couldn't push a run across. In the bottom of the thirteenth, leadoff batter Felix Mantilla reached on an error and went to second on a sacrifice bunt. The perfect game over, Haddix issued an intentional walk to Hank Aaron, before Joe Adcock doubled to center, scoring Mantilla, for the only run of the game—an unearned run.]

That was just a thrill to play in the game. Every out was so easy. It was such an easy game. It was a fun game to play in. And even though we lost, it was a great game.

Well, the 1960 game, they won't let me forget that. That's been pretty good. But I think of Harvey, Harvey Haddix throwing that no-hitter, and Lew Burdette pitched against him and gave up 12 hits or something like that in 13 innings. Lew Burdette called him after the game and said, "Harvey, you got to learn how to spread your hits out." So that was pretty good. It was tough we lost. You'd rather get beat 11–0, 10–0, 16–3, rather than 1–0. If you lose 1–0, you can point fingers—"if I'd done this," or, "if he'd done that," or, "if he'd made this pitch," all that kind of stuff.

In that World Series game, I still don't remember running around the bases. I was just on a cloud floating. I don't think I touched the ground once it went out, and I floated around. It was a high fastball. Ralph Terry threw it. He said it was a slider, but it didn't slide. I don't think I had faced him before that. I don't remember. I remember that part but not too much else. It's been a while, 48 years ago. It's nice when people ask. It's a fun memory. It's not one where you struck out or one went through your legs or you made an error to lose the game or something like that. So it's a fun memory.

Dave Winfield

David Mark Winfield
Born: October 3, 1951, in St. Paul, Minnesota
MLB debut: June 19, 1973
Final game: October 1, 1995
Teams: San Diego Padres (1973–1980), New York Yankees
(1981–1988, 1990), California Angels (1990–1991),
Toronto Blue Jays (1992), Minnesota Twins (1993–1994),
Cleveland Indians (1995)
Primary position: Right field
Bats: Right—**Throws:** Right
Hall of Fame induction: 2001
Vote: 435 votes of 515 ballots cast, 84.47%

One of the most gifted athletes to play the game, Dave Winfield
was born the day Bobby Thomson hit the "Shot Heard 'Round
the World," winning the pennant for the New York Giants.
Winfield was drafted by the Padres in the first round of the
1973 draft out of the University of Minnesota with the fourth
overall pick, one selection behind fellow Hall of Famer Robin
Yount. Winfield was the first athlete to be drafted by four teams
in three different sports—the NFL's Minnesota Vikings, the
NBA's Atlanta Hawks, and the ABA's Utah Stars, along with
the Padres.

He made his big-league debut shortly after the draft, going
1-for-4 with a run scored as the Padres' starting left fielder
against the Astros, joining a select few who never played a
minor-league game. In 56 games that season, Winfield hit

.277 with three home runs and 12 RBIs, playing left field, center, and first base.

In 22 seasons, Winfield hit .283, with a .353 on-base percentage, .475 slugging percentage, 3,110 hits, 465 home runs, 1,833 RBIs, 540 doubles, and 223 stolen bases in 2,973 games. A 12-time All-Star with seven Gold Gloves and six Silver Sluggers, Winfield also had 166 outfield assists, thanks to his strong and accurate arm.

Winfield missed the entire 1989 season with a back injury, but in 1990 was named Comeback Player of the Year. Known throughout his career for his humanitarian efforts, Winfield also finished in the top 10 in MVP voting seven times. In 1999 he was ranked 94th on *The Sporting News* list of 100 Greatest Baseball Players.

It was his strong right arm that would give baseball one of its stranger incidents. In 1983 before the fifth inning in Toronto's Exhibition Stadium with the Yankees, Winfield accidentally killed a seagull with a warm-up throw in the outfield. Nine years later, now playing for the Blue Jays, Winfield gave baseball one of its most memorable moments, this time with his bat. In 1992, in the Jays' first-ever World Series appearance, Winfield's eleventh-inning, two-out, two-RBI double in Game 6 delivered Toronto's first World Series championship.

My favorite has to be when we won the World Series in Toronto and I got a double that drove in the winning runs in the sixth game. Toronto beat the Braves. I think it was just kind of the culmination of everything I had dreamed of playing as a kid, the way we went into our practices each day. Whatever we did when we were kids it was always, alright, you're up to bat, two outs, men on base, last game of the World Series, and you always had to end your practice on the right note. And that is what we did. We'd hit the ball and chase it and then go home. And that's what happened—getting a hit in the World Series and having it make all the difference. And that stands out. Charlie Leibrandt was the pitcher. A lefty, for whatever reason they left him in the game. And I got a hit.

There were great individual games and all that. But this was individual. It was team. It was history. It was a lot of things. So that's the one I remember. People comment that here's a guy—and I was a big guy but I was fast and did a lot of things pretty well out there. My first game in the major leagues. I played the game like I got my first hit in the major leagues. My first hit was a smash off the third baseman's glove, and while he scrambled to get the ball, I'm flying down the first-base line. The throw was high, and I went into first base head first. I did a head-first slide into first base to get my first hit. I just played all out, all out, all the time. And that made a difference. That's the way I played the game. And the most satisfying one was 1992 World Series Game 6.

I stayed in the game. Most of that year I'd been a DH, even though I played some games in the outfield. Cito Gaston was my manager, and he was my teammate when I first came to San Diego. He wanted to know if they were going to take me out for defense in, I can't remember what inning it was. I said, no, let me stay out there. I remember I made a very nice diving catch in the outfield, sinking line drive in right-center. And I caught it and threw it in, like I played good defense my whole career. And I got the chance to get the hit after that.

And I was just so happy for a guy who was my friend, my teammate, my roommate, and now he was my manager. It was an away game. And when you stand in the middle, literally, of a ballpark on second base after driving in a couple runs, and of those 50,000 people maybe 1,000 were cheering and the rest of them were stunned, and you're standing in the middle, you get a great deal of satisfaction.

I wanted that chance because the last time I was in the World Series was 11 years before that. My team didn't win. I didn't do really well. And it was just like, hey, here's another opportunity. So you never know. Because everybody's career isn't like a fairy tale where everything is great. And if you have a long career, you have the ups and downs. It was just very satisfying. It took me about 20 years to get to that point. It was very satisfying. Some guys get it their first year, second year and think it's easy, and it's going to come around all the time. I couldn't have played any better. I wouldn't have approached my game any differently. I wouldn't have been a different person. You just keep giving it your best all the time and just have to hope that things fall into place. And that time they did.

Ozzie Smith

Osborne Earl Smith
Born: December 26, 1954, in Mobile, Alabama
MLB debut: April 7, 1978
Final game: September 29, 1996
Teams: San Diego Padres (1978–1981), St. Louis Cardinals (1982–1996)
Primary position: Shortstop
Bats: Switch—**Throws:** Right
Hall of Fame induction: 2002
Vote: 433 votes of 472 ballots cast, 91.74%

Ozzie Smith's acrobatic fielding gems over 19 seasons supported his reputation as baseball's best defensive shortstop of all time. Drafted by the Padres in 1977, the "Wizard of Oz" debuted as San Diego's starting shortstop the following season, playing in 159 games in 1978, finishing second in National League Rookie of the Year voting.

His backflips in the field at the start of games were just a warm-up for the fielding plays he would make during games. In 1981 he was named to the first of 12 straight All-Star teams, with 15 overall, starting 10 consecutive from 1983 to 1992. He also won 13 consecutive Gold Gloves, from 1980 through 1992.

Traded to the Cardinals before the 1982 season, Ozzie helped St. Louis to its first World Series championship since 1967, the first of four postseasons with the Cardinals, also giving St. Louis NL pennants in 1985 and 1987, and a NL Central title in 1996.

In 1987, arguably his best offensive season, Smith finished second in MVP voting, batting .303 with 75 RBIs, 40 doubles, 104 runs scored, and 43 stolen bases, playing 158 games and winning the Silver Slugger award.

In 19 seasons, Smith hit .262 with 28 home runs, 402 doubles, 69 triples, 793 RBIs, and 580 stolen bases in 9,396 at-bats over 2,573 games.

Upon his retirement after the 1996 season at the age of 41, Ozzie had set major-league records at shortstop for assists (8,375); double plays (1,590); total chances (12,624), seasons with 500 or more assists (8); most seasons leading the league in assists (8); and most seasons leading the league in chances, with eight. He led the NL in fielding percentage eight times and had a career mark of .978, the fifth-best of all time, all while playing shortstop.

In the strike-shortened 1981 season he led the league in games (110), at-bats (450), and plate appearances (507). He also led the league in sacrifice hits in 1978 (28), and 1980 (23); and at-bats per strikeouts in 1986 (19.0) and 1993 (30.3).

In 1999 Smith was ranked 87th on *The Sporting News* list of 100 Greatest Baseball Players, and in 2007 was named the shortstop on Rawlings' All-Time Gold Glove team.

In 1985 Ozzie was named MVP of the NLCS, hitting .435, with a .500 on-base percentage, .696 slugging percentage, with 10 hits (including a double, a triple, and a home run), three RBIs, and four runs scored in six games against the Dodgers. The home run, a walk-off solo shot in Game 5, was his only roundtripper in 42 postseason games and was his first as a left-handed batter in 3,009 at-bats.

While it may be difficult for Smith to pick a particular moment from his career, that home run, with legendary broadcaster Jack Buck telling fans, "Go crazy, folks! Go crazy!" was later voted by fans as the greatest moment in Busch Stadium history.

I don't know if there's a favorite, because I think as a player you go out and you play every day. The goal every day is to make today as good as yesterday was. Or, if it was a bad game, better than yesterday was. And I think a guy who is really into his craft, you don't really have time for that. It's like fielding a groundball or making a great play. If you make a great play, you have to get rid of it as quickly as possible, just like a bad play. You got to get rid of it as quickly as possible because the next one might be the one that determines whether you win or lose.

So that was pretty much the way it was. You play every day, you lay it on the line every day, and when you walk away, hopefully it gives you a feeling of completion, a feeling of accomplishment. There were many days that I went out and I played where I did not play the way that I wanted to. But when I asked myself the question, "Did I do the best I could today?" the answer for 19 years was yes. And beyond that, there's nothing else. You can't beat yourself up about not being able to go out because the other guys are out there trying, too. So you're not going to be the blessed one every day. All I could do was make sure I did and gave my all everyday.

But in 1985, the home run in 1985, it was at that point I think people started looking at me as much more than just a defensive player. And it's all of our goal to be as

Ozzie Smith pumps his fist while he runs the bases after his ninth-inning game-winning home run on October 15, 1985, against the Dodgers in the NLCS.

well-rounded as we could be. So that was a feeling of accomplishment. Yet I continued to work hard, and did that because of my work ethic. I had learned the fundamentals of hitting. My defensive prowess had allowed me to remain at the big-league level to learn it here. And it wasn't easy learning against the likes of Nolan Ryan, Fergie Jenkins, Tom Seaver, Steve Carlton. The list just goes on and on. So it was really a feeling of accomplishment when it was all over because I kind of had to do it the hard way.

But hearing Jack Buck say, "Go crazy," that's pretty neat. You never know when one of those moments is going to come. So I feel very fortunate to have been in a situation where you could have someone like a Jack Buck be a part of. It's been part of history for Cardinals fans. It's been voted the number one play of the last 20 years or something. So it's nice to be able to be in a situation like that where you are a part of a very famous call.

Gary Carter

Gary Edmund Carter
Born: April 8, 1954, in Culver City, California
MLB debut: September 16, 1974
Final game: September 27, 1992
Teams: Montreal Expos (1974–1984, 1992), New York Mets
(1985–1989), San Francisco Giants (1990), Los Angeles
Dodgers (1991)
Primary position: Catcher
Bats: Right—**Throws:** Right
Hall of Fame induction: 2003
Vote: 387 votes of 496 ballots cast, 78.02%

Selected by the Montreal Expos in the third round of the 1972 draft—the same round in which fellow future Hall of Famer Dennis Eckersley was chosen—Gary Carter would go on to inherit the mantle of best catcher in the National League from Johnny Bench, as that future Hall of Famer's career was winding down.

An 11-time All-Star, including his rookie season when he was named The Sporting News Rookie of the Year. Carter earned five Silver Slugger and three Gold Glove Awards. He was named the All-Star Game's MVP twice, in 1981, going 2-for-3, with two home runs in the NL's 5–4 win, and in 1984, with a solo homer in the NL's 3–1 victory.

In 1981 Carter helped the Expos to their first postseason berth, hitting .421 with two home runs and six RBIs in the NLDS against the Phillies, and .438 in the NLCS against the Dodgers. On his Hall of Fame plaque Carter is wearing a Montreal Expos cap, the first and likely last player so depicted, as the Expos moved to Washington, D.C., and became the Nationals before the 2005 season.

In 1977 Carter hit the first of his four consecutive Opening Day home runs, a solo shot in the sixth inning that provided the difference in the Expos' 4–3 win over the Phillies.

In 1984 Carter had arguably his finest offensive season, posting career highs in games (159), at-bats (596), hits (175), average (.294), and total bases (290), and a league-best 106 RBIs.

He was traded to the Mets after that season, and hit another Opening Day home run in 1985, this time a tenth-inning, game-winning homer.

In 19 seasons, Carter, known as "Kid," compiled a career hitting mark of .262 with 2,092 hits, 324 home runs, 1,225 RBIs, and 1,025 runs scored. He produced nine 20-home-run seasons, two 30-homer seasons, and four 100-RBI seasons. Upon retiring, Carter had caught 2,056 games with 11,785 putouts, another NL record. He had an impressive .991 fielding percentage behind the plate, with just 121 errors and never more than 10 in a season. He also played right field, first base, left field, and third base in his career.

With the Mets he gave baseball one of its most memorable moments. Although he hit two home runs in Game 4 of the 1986 World Series against the Red Sox, it is the dramatic comeback the Mets staged in Game 6 that stands out. Down two runs in the tenth inning, Carter's single ignited the rally to give the Mets the incredible win, forcing a decisive Game 7 showdown against Boston.

After the Red Sox took a two-run lead in the top of the inning, Carter's two-out single was followed by singles from Kevin Mitchell and Ray Knight, scoring Carter. A wild pitch by Bob Stanley scored Mitchell, and Mookie Wilson's grounder between first baseman Bill Buckner's legs scored Knight, giving the Mets the win and baseball fans an indelible memory.

Game 6 of the 1986 World Series, without a doubt. I won All-Star MVPs in 1981 and 1984, and those were great. But nothing compares to Game 6. There's so many things that transpired. When Dave Henderson hit the home run in the tenth and then we were down 5–3 and thinking, "Oh, my goodness. This could be the end." In Game 6, I remember I was given the hit sign with a 3–0 count with the bases loaded, and hit that line drive to Jim Rice to drive in Mazzilli to tie the game up in the eighth. There were so many exciting things that happened in that game. So how can you count that out, that it was truly an exciting game? That's kind of the way I look at it.

That game just stands out so much. It does, and the reason is because it meant so much. It got us one step closer to winning a world championship. You can have great games during the course of a season, but that doesn't get you to where you ultimately want to be, and that's a world champion. There's no comparison. I remember having a three-homer game in San Diego [in 1985] and the next day I came back and hit two more, and I tied a major-league record for hitting five home runs in two days. And when I look at stuff like that I say, well, yeah, that was all great and it was nice individually. But you're ultimately trying to get to your goal, and that's to win a World Series. That's why that game sticks out the most. It's the one that's talked about the most and it's the one that's most remembered.

Jim Rice of the Red Sox is tagged out at the plate by the Mets' Gary Carter in the seventh inning of Game 6 of the 1986 World Series on October 25.

People ask, "Well, how was it?" First they get names wrong, a lot of the time. Then they ask something like, "Oh, were you the one that scored the winning run?" No, that was Ray Knight. "Was Keith Hernandez really in the clubhouse drinking a beer and smoking a cigar?" Well, yeah, he was. "Was Kevin Mitchell in the clubhouse trying to make phone reservations for an airline flight out the next day?" Yeah, he was. Those kinds of questions. There's a lot of things that come up. But ultimately, when you're in the game, you don't even think about all those extra things. Or, how about the parachutist that came down in the first couple of innings. He was coming down to try and inspire us. Those kind of things. I mean, he gets arrested because obviously that can't be done. Well, where did the plane come from? Somewhere, but this guy came out of nowhere. And the plane left the LaGuardia Airport. How did some small aircraft get through the radar? You know, just crazy stuff. So how can it not be the most memorable, especially in the fashion in which we did win it? Throughout my career I had a lot of exciting games. But there's nothing—all pale in comparison to that game because it was just one that everybody continues to talk about, and we're talking 22 years later.

After that game was over, I knew we would win the World Series. No doubt in my mind, with the way we had done it all year. We were the cardiac kids. My goodness, all the ninth-inning comebacks and everything else. I just felt very strongly that it was going to happen. There was no question in my mind.

We were down 3–0 in Game 7, I realize that. But it didn't faze us because we really felt like we were the team of destiny that year. And that was the case.

We had the momentum and the confidence. That's exactly it. But the other, too, was we were rained out on Game 7. So it gave everybody an extra day's rest. So everybody was basically equal. The advantage that we had was that we were the home team, playing in our home ballpark. So that goes without saying. When you've got that home-field advantage and it's a crucial, meaningful game, I'm telling you it makes all the difference in the world to have the home-team advantage. That's why if you look on the record, home-field advantage and how teams play at home, you should play above .500. They always say you play .600 at home and .500 on the road and you got a good chance to win.

Thinking back to that game, it is clear to a certain extent. Other things have been brought to my attention about things that transpired. There was even a book written about that series and many others. But it just talked about all the little scenarios that occurred. So, yeah, it's the freshest in my mind. It was without a doubt the most exciting. There's nothing much more to say except every time I run into people or go to card shows or different things like that, people always bring up Game 6 and the 1986 Mets.

There's no question reactions from Mets fans are different than Red Sox fans. But you know what? Red Sox fans are very gracious because they're great baseball fans. And all the Boston fans that I run into say, "Oh, you did it to my Red Sox." And I say, "Well, yeah, but it just wasn't meant to be, and I know you guys were looking to break the curse." But look what has happened recently. They've won two of the last four years. So think of it in a positive way. They've won more championships in their franchise's history than the Mets have. They've only won twice. So that's all a lot of people have to go on, is that '86 team. So that's where it's at.

Eddie Murray

Eddie Clarence Murray
Born: February 24, 1956, in Los Angeles, California
MLB debut: April 7, 1977
Final game: September 20, 1997
Teams: Baltimore Orioles (1977–1988, 1996), Los Angeles
    Dodgers (1989–1991, 1997), New York Mets (1992–1993),
    Cleveland Indians (1994–1996), Anaheim Angels (1997)
Primary position: First base
Bats: Switch—**Throws:** Right
Hall of Fame induction: 2003
Vote: 423 votes of 496 ballots cast, 85.28%

After being drafted in the third round of the 1973 draft out
of Locke High School in Los Angeles, where he was teammates with fellow future Hall of Famer Ozzie Smith, Eddie
Murray quickly established himself as one of the most consistent and dominating switch-hitters in the game. He was
named Rookie of the Year in 1977, hitting .283 with a .470
slugging percentage, 173 hits, 27 home runs, and 88 RBIs
playing in 160 total games, as the designated hitter, first
baseman, and left fielder.

His consistency and durability earned him the nickname
"Steady Eddie" throughout his 21-season career. In his
second season he nearly duplicated those numbers, hitting
.285, with 174 hits, a .480 slugging percentage, 27 home
runs, and 95 RBIs in 161 games. He drove in at least 75 runs
in each of his first 20 seasons, and had six 100-RBI seasons,

while playing at least 150 games in 16 seasons, and hitting .300 or better in seven seasons.

In more than 21 seasons, Murray hit .287 with 504 home runs, 1,917 RBIs, 560 doubles, a .359 on-base percentage, .476 slugging percentage, and 222 intentional walks in 3,026 games and 11,336 at-bats. Upon retiring, he was the all-time career leader among switch-hitters in RBIs and second to Mickey Mantle in home runs. He was the third player, with Willie Mays and Hank Aaron, to accumulate 3,000 hits and 500 home runs. His 19 grand slams are third all-time, behind Lou Gehrig and Manny Ramirez, and he hit home runs from each side of the plate in 11 games, a record tied by Chili Davis in 1997.

An eight-time All-Star, Murray won Gold Gloves in 1982, 1983, and 1984 and Silver Sluggers in 1983 and 1984. He finished in the top 10 in MVP voting eight times. He holds the major-league record for games played, at 2,413, and assists, with 1,865, for a first baseman.

In 1999 he was ranked 77th on the list of Baseball's 100 Greatest Players compiled by *The Sporting News.*

A three-homer game—a two-run shot shy of the home-run cycle—going 4-for-5 with nine RBIs, a walk, and a single, while giving a family friend a birthday surprise on August 26, 1985, is an easy one to remember for Murray.

A game in Anaheim. I had three home runs. I hit everything that day but a two-run homer, and I remember flying out on the warning track in center field with one on. That was nice because it was home. You had everybody there. I'll never forget. We had the actress Emma Samms. She had never seen a baseball game. They're trying to throw a party for her, and it started off with her people calling me and saying, "She needs to go on this day so we can do the party." And that day, she's trying to throw a monkey wrench in it because I think she had other plans. So, anyway, I talked to her. I said, "I know I'm going to have a good game. So you got to come out this day." And she came out and she's sitting up there with my family. And I ended up hitting three home runs, and then I flew out on the warning track the one time I would have hit a two-run homer. I hit a grand slam, a three-run homer, and a solo. The last time up I had a chance to do it again. I hit the ball out of the park but I missed the foul pole by about four feet. And then he walked me. And I'll never forget, Reggie Jackson and, I think, Bobby Grich were in the papers for just, I think, saying that their pitcher was a little gutless. After I missed that foul ball, he wasn't going to throw another strike. Yeah, I won't mention his name.

I knew [Emma Samms]. But her PR people and her agent, I knew all of them, and they were just trying to do something behind her back [to surprise her], and they said, "Well, you're coming to town. Why don't you try to get her to go to a ballgame and then we can throw the party?"

My family was there, too. I can remember that that Baltimore team was 350-something tickets over because I think we had 13 or 14 guys from the Southern California area.

It was just special. That was it. I guess she thought it happened all the time.

Dennis Eckersley

Dennis Lee Eckersley
Born: October 3, 1954, in Oakland, California
MLB debut: April 12, 1975
Final game: September 26, 1998
Teams: Cleveland Indians (1975–1977), Boston Red Sox
(1978–1984, 1998), Chicago Cubs (1984–1986), Oakland
A's (1987–1995), St. Louis Cardinals (1996–1997)
Primary position: Pitcher
Bats: Right—**Throws:** Right
Hall of Fame induction: 2004
Vote: 421 votes of 506 ballots cast, 83.2%

One of the most colorful and successful pitchers in baseball history, Dennis Eckersley had a unique career. Drafted by the Indians in the third round of the 1972 draft—the same round in which fellow future Hall of Famer Gary Carter was selected—Eckersley spent the first half of his 24-season career primarily as a successful starter and the second half as one of the game's most dominant relievers.

He was the first pitcher to have a 20-win season and a 50-save season in his career. He is the only pitcher with 100 complete games and 200 saves.

In 1975 Eckersley earned American League Rookie Pitcher of the Year honors, posting a record of 13–7, with a 2.60 ERA in 34 games, and 24 starts, with two shutouts, six complete games, two saves, 152 strikeouts, and 90 walks in 187 innings.

After a trade to the Red Sox before the 1978 season, Eckersley had his most successful season as a starter, with a record of 20–8, 2.99 ERA, with 16 complete games, three shutouts, 162 strikeouts, and 71 walks in a career-high 268 innings.

A six-time All-Star who was ranked 98th on the list of Baseball's 100 Greatest Players compiled by *The Sporting News,* Eckersley's career as a reliever was launched when he was traded from the Cubs to the A's in 1987. From 1988 through 1992, he was the most dominant closer in baseball, with 220 saves. In 1988 he earned ALCS MVP honors, with four saves in Oakland's sweep of Boston. In 1990 he was the only reliever in history with more saves than base runners allowed—48 saves, compared to 41 hits, four walks, no hit batters, posting a 0.61 ERA. In 1992 he earned the AL Cy Young and MVP Awards, going 7–1 with 51 saves and a 1.91 ERA. He had 93 K's and 11 walks, six of which were intentional.

Throughout his career, Eckersley led the league in several categories as both a starter and a reliever, including saves in 1988 (45) and 1992 (51); walks per nine innings in 1986 (1.93); strikeouts-to-walks ratio in 1977 (3.54), 1982 (2.95), and 1985 (6.16); and games finished in 1992 (65).

Upon his retirement, Eckersley had compiled a record of 197–171 with a 3.50 ERA, 390 saves, 2,401 strikeouts, and 738 walks in 1,071 games spanning 3,285⅔ innings.

While others may remember the home run he gave up to Kirk Gibson in Game 1 of the 1988 World Series, Eckersley also helped his teams to six division titles, a wild-card berth, three league pennants, and a World Series championship with the A's in 1989, when he posted a save in the Series-clinching Game 4.

With all his accomplishment as both a starter and reliever in his lengthy career, Eckersley remembers a game early in his career, May 30, 1977, pitching for the Indians against the Angels, when he accomplished one of the rarest and most difficult feats for a pitcher.

It's hard to pick one game, because one game would be a personal one, like throwing the no-hitter. Another game would be like catching the last out of the World Series. Or a devastating loss, like the Kirk Gibson thing— not that I want that one to be the most memorable, it just happens to be because of what it meant: that was the World Series.

But I guess if I was going to pick one, it was early on. I threw a no-hitter when I was, like, 22, and at the time it was the biggest thing that I'd ever had happen because it wasn't like you were going to be on a team that you know you're going to go to the playoffs and that whole thing. It was very personal. It was not a team thing. But at the time it was huge. You finally get some attention playing in Cleveland, and that's the only way you could do it.

It was against the Angels and Frank Tanana. He was probably the best left-hander in the game at the time. Then he got hurt after that. They had a good lineup, predominantly right-handed, which was helpful, not to take anything away from the performance!

At that time, when I was that age, I wanted to throw a no-hitter every time I pitched. That's how goofy I was, I'm not kidding! Not every time. Sometimes I knew I wasn't throwing real well. But for the most part, I always felt

Indians pitcher Dennis Eckersley poses during spring training in Miami, Florida, in March 1978.

good and maybe a little naïve. But to me, that kind of thinking is a good way to begin, thinking you don't want to get hit at all. I used to think I had that kind of stuff. So the confidence was there. I used to get mad every time somebody would get a hit, whatever start it was. I thought I was going to throw one every night.

I think once you throw one, it's not on your [mind]. It goes away. I think the desire is there, but you have to be so fortunate anyway. But to be really honest, the stars have to be aligned. [The Angels] had Joe Rudi, Don Baylor, Bobby Bonds, Willie Aikens, Dave Chalk, Bobby Grich. So that's five right-handed hitters. That was a pretty good club. Jerry Remy was the second baseman.

I didn't really think I had something extra that day. Not necessarily. But you know you're pitching against a good pitcher. You know you can't give up anything. That's when you see a lot of guys have good performances. They match up. They know they have to pitch well.

I started getting nervous probably in the sixth, seventh inning. We got a run in the first inning I remember. I was yelling at Tanana—I used to do that sort of thing. I was just trying to rattle him somehow to get a run off of him. You could hear everything in the dugout, because there was nobody there. It was Memorial Day. There was only, like, 13,000 people there. He probably looked at me, but I do recall yelling at him. But we did get one! And it held.

In the ninth inning, I remember that's as intense as I've ever been on the mound to that point. And after I got the second out, I was pointing. I figured if I was going to do it, I might as well do it in style. I remember getting the ball back from Buddy Bell, the third baseman. And I was pointing at him, "One more." And as I got back on the mound, the last hitter was a guy named Gil Flores. And nobody had heard his name. I remember the last out. The game was not on TV, obviously, in 1977. Photographers used to kind of bother you a little bit because they didn't just shoot from the camera wells. They'd come out a little bit. So it was distracting, not for me, but for the hitter. The hitter got in and kept backing out [of the batter's box] because something was distracting him, and it was the cameras. So this is when I went off. I was yelling at the guy, telling him, "Get in there!" I was telling him, "They're not here to take *your* picture!" I was crazy. And the funny part of this was Jerry Remy was on deck watching this. So I ended up striking him out. But the next thing you know, I was sort of left with, "Oh, he points at everybody and tells them to get in there." Like I did this every day. It's crazy. You'd think that I was Nolan Ryan or something.

But that was what ended up happening, because the guy was taking forever to get in there. Of all times, right? And that's why I was screaming. I was anxious. I'm always anxious, let alone with one more out. So that's kind of a memorable moment.

I guess, for that time, and being in Cleveland, there was some media attention after the game. I was on a string of 21⅔ hitless innings. The game before, I pitched 12 innings and the last seven were no-no. And then I threw a no-no, so that's 16. I think it was the last 7 of the 12-inning game, and then the no-no, that's 16, and then I went the next game 5⅔ no-no. And then Ruppert Jones took me deep. I was on a roll.

I was feeling invincible. Absolutely. It wasn't like I was striking everybody out, but it was like magic. So that's why that is memorable. It was a magical time, magical streak.

After the no-hitter, there was a bit of a letdown. But at the same time, I had this streak. I couldn't help but see how far it would go. Then I went to Seattle. I had never pitched in a dome because there were no domes. It was the eeriest place. If you've never been in a dome, for the first time, imagine that. The first time you're in a dome and you've got a 16 job running. And anybody could go deep at any given time there.

Any time you get a no-hitter, it's Johnny Vander Meer time. But I had my own little thing going in. So I couldn't help but be aware of it. At that time it was the biggest thing going. The thing about it is that's what I was sort of known for in Cleveland. I only spent three years there, but that was a big part of it, the no-hitter. You're remembered for something like that, regardless of if you're an obscure pitcher.

That's the easiest one to talk about. The other one is ugly. But when you look back at your career, you remember the bad ones. You really do, especially pitching in that venue. Because they're devastating. A no-hitter is one thing, because how many no-hitters are there? The biggest ones are the ones where there's a devastating loss. It's funny when you look back over your career, those are the ones that stick out. Those are the ones you're left with, if you're lucky enough to be on that stage. And I have good stuff on that stage, too, winning the whole thing, being MVP of the playoffs. So I have good stuff. But the losses, you remember, I don't know what it is. Because it's such a big responsibility. You're left with what's left.

Is it tough to talk about? Oh, God, no, because I have to all the time. Almost every year it comes up again. It's easy to talk about. When I do go speaking, it's a big part of my story because a lot of growth comes out of defeat, it really does. You find out a lot about yourself. You really do. Not that I wanted to learn like that. But it builds character.

Paul Molitor

Paul Leo Molitor
Born: August 22, 1956, in St. Paul, Minnesota
MLB debut: April 7, 1978
Final game: September 27, 1998
Teams: Milwaukee Brewers (1978–1992), Toronto Blue Jays
(1993–1995), Minnesota Twins (1996–1998)
Primary position: Designated hitter
Bats: Right—Throws: Right
Hall of Fame induction: 2004
Vote: 431 votes of 506 ballots cast, 85.2%

Selected out of the University of Minnesota by Milwaukee
with the third pick in the 1977 draft, Paul Molitor made his
debut as the Brewers' Opening Day shortstop the next
season, getting a hit and an RBI. In the next game, he
added three hits and five RBIs, and was on his way to a 21-
season career built on versatility, consistency, savvy, and
clutch-hitting.

A seven-time All-Star and four-time Silver Slugger winner,
Molitor played 791 games at third base, 400 at second, 197
at first, 57 at short, 44 in center field, four in right, and four in
left, while serving as the designated hitter in 1,174 games.

In his 21 seasons, "Molly," "the Ignitor," hit .306 with
3,319 hits, 605 doubles, 114 triples, 234 home runs, 1,307
RBIs, and 504 stolen bases in 2,683 games and 10,835
at-bats.

Molitor led the league in runs scored in 1982 (136), 1987 (114), and 1991 (133); plate appearances in 1982 (751), 1991 (749), and 1993 (725); at-bats in 1982 (666) and 1991 (665); games played in 1994 (115); hits in 1991 (216), 1993 (211), and 1996 (225); doubles in 1987 (41); triples in 1991 (13); and singles in 1994 (107) and 1996 (167).

Upon retiring, Molly was just the fourth player with at least 3,000 hits, a .300 lifetime average, and 500 stolen bases. He was the only player to reach those marks while also hitting at least 200 home runs.

In 1999 he was ranked 99th on the list of Baseball's 100 Greatest Players compiled by *The Sporting News*.

In 1987 he hit in 39 consecutive games, the seventh-longest streak of all time. With his hometown Twins, Molitor recorded his 3,000th hit, the only player to do so by hitting a triple. In 1996 he became the first 40-year-old player with at least 200 hits in a season, 225 actually, since Sam Rice reached that plateau in 1930.

In 1981 and 1982 he helped the Brewers into the post-season, including the '82 World Series against the Cardinals. Although the Brewers lost in seven games, Molitor had five hits in Game 1, establishing a one-game Series record.

In 29 playoff games over three postseasons, he hit .368 with a .615 slugging percentage, six home runs, 22 RBIs, and 28 runs scored. In 13 World Series games, he hit .418, with a .636 slugging percentage, two home runs, 11 RBIs, and 15 runs scored.

In 1993, in his first season with the Blue Jays after 15 seasons in Milwaukee, Molitor got back to the World Series for the first time since 1982. He tied a World Series record, hitting .500, going 12-for-24, with a .571 on-base percentage, 1.000 slugging percentage, two home runs, and eight

RBIs, earning Series MVP honors as the Blue Jays beat the Phillies, with his father in the stands for the clinching Game 6.

There're a lot of different reasons you remember games. And actually when you're young and playing for state championships and College World Series and things like that, they seem very significant at the time—and they were. And, of course, your first big-league game, and there's a lot of memorable individual performances along the way. But the game for me that is my favorite game is so because I was able to do something only one time in my career—play in a game where I was a member of the team that won that game and the world championship. The 1993 World Series Game 6 was my most memorable game as a major league player for a few reasons. I had played in one World Series prior, in 1982, as a young player, somewhat naïve in assuming that I'd have more chances. We lost in seven and had to wait 11 more years and changed teams before I got another opportunity.

And at 37 years old, I didn't know if it would be my last, but I'd kind of made an effort heading into that World Series to do a much better job of trying to savor the visual pictures. Being removed from 1982 was something that I really didn't...I remembered 1982 and I know the disappointment, but it was a little fuzzy. So there was a conscious effort to try to take it all in the best I could, and it really helped me try to slow the Series down mentally and probably added to my ability to play somewhat well in that Series.

But that particular game we had just come off Game 5 when Curt Schilling had shut us out in Philadelphia to keep the Series alive for the Phillies and bring it to 3–2, and we headed back home to Toronto. The game unfolded in our favor in a lot of ways. We got a lead early. I think we had three in the first, and I was part of the rally in that inning. I hit a triple.

Later in the game, Dave Stewart was pitching for us and was dominating early. We built the lead to 5–1. I hit a home run in the game. And then the Phillies mounted a comeback. Stewart tired, and our bullpen didn't hold the lead, and we end up falling behind 6–5.

And, as confident as we were, we were not too excited about the possibility of squandering a 3–1 Series edge and letting the Phillies get back to even. And who knows what can happen in a Game 7 situation. In the ninth inning, Mitch Williams, who had had a great year but a somewhat tough Series, came in to try to close out the game. We had the top of the lineup come up to start the inning with Rickey Henderson, the best leadoff hitter of all time. And sure enough, he works Mitch for a walk. Devon White, who was hitting second, had a great at-bat, a lot of pitches, but ended up flying out to left field. I followed Devon. And an interesting sidebar to this story is that for most youngsters who have a passion for baseball at some point in their backyard career, they envision a scenario where they have a chance to come up and hit a home run and win a World Series in the bottom of the ninth inning. And I remember thinking about that in the on-deck circle. I almost had to resist the temptation to linger on that thought because that certainly wasn't my game, and my chance to get a hit off Mitch Williams was a lot better than it was of hitting a home run off Mitch Williams. So this was the one opportunity I had in my career to fulfill that boyhood fantasy and yet I tried to fight the urge to swing for the fences. Plus, I hadn't done very well off Mitch in the past. But I hit a line drive to center, and Rickey stopped at second. The SkyDome was going a little bit crazy, and sure enough Joe Carter, who had a couple of feeble swings early in the count, and then somewhat flat-footed golfed a slider down the left-field line.

And I remember, as I ran toward second base, watching Pete Incaviglia go after the ball. But if somehow that ball got over his head or hit off the wall, if I could score, I was the winning run. But right as I was rounding second base, I saw the ball disappear over the left-field wall and was able to enjoy that last 180 feet around the bases as the place exploded. After 16 years as a major-league player, I was able to enter the winner's circle.

A lot had happened that year, the transition in Toronto after 15 years in Milwaukee, questioning myself in spring training and the early parts of the season if I had made the right decision. And five or six months removed, to be a part of that celebration on the field and be embraced by the Toronto fans, and finally become a world champion for that particular season are a lot of the reasons why that game stands out for me.

I can remember all the at-bats in that game. Not in a bullshit way but just as an indication of the vision I had. I remember when I hit a home run late in the game to increase our lead, I knew where my dad was sitting. And for me to have the presence of mind, rounding second base to look over there and try to make eye contact with my dad. And I was able to pick him out of the crowd. So I didn't do anything, but it was just a nice thing. I knew it meant a lot to him to be there. So, yeah, I can picture things. I hear the fireworks going off.

I saw the look on my dad's face. He was cheering. He was never the rah-rah kind of guy. But I just remember making eye contact with him. I don't know if it ever happened before. It probably did. He used to sit behind home plate once in a while. But this particular game, he was more down the third-base line. So it just kind of worked out where that thought kind of popped into my head as I was running, because I usually ran with my head down when I hit one of those rare home runs, and I just thought of it as I approached it and just glanced up and knew where he was at. So that was kind of a cool moment.

Wade Boggs

Wade Anthony Boggs
Born: June 15, 1958, in Omaha, Nebraska
MLB debut: April 10, 1982
Final game: August 27, 1999
Teams: Boston Red Sox (1982–1992), New York Yankees
(1993–1997), Tampa Bay Devil Rays (1998–1999)
Primary position: Third base
Bats: Left—**Throws:** Right
Hall of Fame induction: 2005
Vote: 474 votes of 516 ballots cast, 91.9%

Drafted out of Plant High School in Tampa in the seventh round of the 1976 draft—the same round in which fellow future Hall of Famer Ozzie Smith was selected (but didn't sign with the Tigers)—Wade Boggs spent six seasons in the minor leagues before establishing himself as one of baseball's most disciplined hitters with a commanding knowledge of the strike zone throughout his 18-season career.

A 12-time All-Star with two Gold Gloves and eight Silver Sluggers, Boggs hit .328 with 3,010 hits, 578 doubles, 118 home runs, and 1,014 RBIs in 9,180 at-bats over 2,440 games. Consistent and methodical, he hit .300 or better in 15 seasons, walked 100 or more times in four straight seasons, scored 100 or more runs in seven straight seasons, hit 40 or more doubles eight times, including seven consecutive seasons. He is the only hitter in the 20th century to post seven consecutive seasons of 200 or more hits.

Boggs won batting titles in 1983 (.361), 1985 (.368), 1986 (.357), 1987 (.363), and 1988 (.366). He led the league in on-base percentage in 1983 (.444), 1985 (.450), 1986 (.453), 1987 (.461), 1988 (.476), and 1989 (.430); plate appearances in 1985 (758), 1988 (719), and 1989 (742); runs in 1988 (128) and 1989 (113); hits in 1985 (240); doubles in 1988 (45) and 1989 (51); walks in 1986 (105) and 1988 (125); singles in 1983 (154), 1984 (162), and 1985 (187); times on base in 1983 (303), 1984 (292), 1985 (340), 1986 (312), 1987 (307), 1988 (342), 1989 (319), and 1990 (275); and intentional walks in 1987 (19), 1988 (18), 1989 (19), 1990 (19), 1991 (25), and 1992 (19).

In 1998, joining his hometown expansion Devil Rays, Boggs hit a home run for his first hit with his new team and the franchise's first-ever homer. In 1999 he became the first player to record his 3,000[th] career hit with a home run.

In 1996 he won a World Series with the Yankees. In Game 4 he drew a tenth-inning walk to force in the go-ahead run, tying the Series against the Braves at two games each. He celebrated the Yankees' first World Series in 18 years by riding a police horse, with the officer, around Yankee Stadium. A far different memory from 10 years earlier.

In 11 seasons with the Red Sox, Boggs never won a World Series, despite three trips to the postseason, including a gut-wrenching loss to the Mets in the 1986 Series. That loss closed a painful season for Boggs, whose mother was killed in a car accident in June of that year. When he returned from her funeral, the Sox were playing the Yankees at Fenway Park.

Probably the game that is most significant to me is when I came back after the death of my mother in 1986; we were playing the Yankees. I had come back on Sunday, and about halfway through the game I got dressed and walked into the dugout, and John Mc-Namara said, "Boggsie, we don't need you today, but just let me know when you're ready to play." And I said, "Well, I'm ready to go whenever you want me to." And that Monday I played. When I walked up to the plate, everyone stood and started clapping. It lasted for about five minutes, and they wouldn't stop. And it really made me feel good. So it was not an individual performance that I had. But it was just how the fans reacted after something that was so tragic.

It was hard to go out and play, but it was something that I needed to do. And I used "in between the lines" to get away from it. Then, once the World Series was over in 1986, that was the scene that everyone saw in the dugout of, "Well, now it's finally over and I have to go home." But it was an outlet that I needed to get away from everything, and I sort of used baseball that way.

I knew my mother was with me that day. Every day she is. Every day.

June 17 [1986] is the worst day of my life, then October 27 was the next-worst night, because I had to deal with [Mets reliever] Jesse Orosco throwing his glove up [and celebrating]. And I knew I had to go home, and I knew my mom wasn't going to be there. Those two dates are etched in stone for me, moments that I have to deal with every day of my life. That just crushes you when you think about it. It's extremely hard. These are things that you try to deal with and get through in your life, and when everyone says, "Remember when?" it's hard. The pain never leaves. I'm never going to *not* think about my mother. I wake up thinking about her. I just wanted to keep playing, just like the movie *Groundhog Day*, because if I stopped, then I had to go home, and my mom wasn't go to be there.

When you look at that 1986 team, that was a helluva team. We accomplished a lot of things that year that a lot of people didn't realize. It exceeded everyone's expectations, not only the fans'. The one thing we had together is we knew we could win and we had a great bunch of guys that year. June 17 really changed my life that year, and these guys were behind me the whole way and just made me feel so special. They said, "Hey, we'll pull through this."

For a favorite memory, that's tough to say. I would probably have to say riding the horse. That was so special, and what we did not accomplish in 1986 I finally accomplished in 1996. But I would say probably the most memorable moment is when I got the call in Yankee Stadium on June 17 when my mom died, and I was in the clubhouse. I remember the time. I remember where I was. It was a tough year, when Jesse Orosco threw the glove up and everything.

When I think about the World Series, the first thing I think of is riding the horse. That was in 1996, and the other one was 1986 watching the Mets celebrate on the pitcher's mound. Those are probably the two most vivid memories that I have of the World Series and October and that time of year. One's as top of the mountain as you can go, and the other's as low as the bottom of the sea as you can go. So completely opposite.

Ryne Sandberg

Ryne Dee Sandberg
Born: September 18, 1959, in Spokane, Washington
MLB debut: September 2, 1981
Final game: September 28, 1997
Teams: Philadelphia Phillies (1981), Chicago Cubs
  (1982–1994, 1996–1997)
Primary position: Second base
Bats: Right—**Throws:** Right
Hall of Fame induction: 2005
Vote: 393 votes of 516 ballots cast, 76.2%

Although Ryne Sandberg was drafted by the Phillies out of North Central High School in Spokane, it was with the Cubs that he established himself as one of the game's best second basemen, with great range, a strong arm, and good power.

Making his major-league debut in 1981 with the Phillies as a pinch runner, and then in the field as a shortstop, the Cubs acquired Sandberg in a trade before the 1982 season, when he primarily played third base, moving to second base for good the next season.

In 16 seasons, "Ryno" hit .285 with 2,386 hits, 403 doubles, 282 home runs, 1,061 RBIs, 1,318 runs scored, and 344 stolen bases in 8,385 at-bats over 2,164 games, fielding at a .989 clip at second, third, and short. He led NL second baseman in assists in seven seasons, fielding percentage in four seasons, and total chances in four seasons.

In 1984 Sandberg earned National League MVP honors, hitting .314 with a .520 slugging percentage, 200 hits, 36 doubles, 19 triples, 19 home runs, 84 RBIs, 114 runs scored, and 32 stolen bases in 156 games. He also played a stellar second base, with a .993 fielding percentage, compared to the league average of .979.

That year he led the Cubs to their first postseason since 1945. Although the Cubs lost the NLCS to the Padres, Sandberg hit .368. In 10 postseason games, he hit .385 (15-for-39), with five doubles, a triple, a home run, nine runs scored, and six RBIs.

In 1990 he was just the third second baseman to reach the 40-homer plateau, joining Rogers Hornsby, who accomplished the feat in 1922, and Davey Johnson, who did so in 1973.

A 10-time All-Star, Sandberg earned nine Gold Gloves and seven Silver Sluggers. From 1989 through 1990 he established a new record for second baseman with 123 consecutive error-free games. Upon retiring, Ryno held records for second baseman with 277 home runs and a .989 fielding percentage.

Although he retired briefly after the 1994 season, in 1996 he returned for two more seasons, hitting 25 home runs and fielding at a .991 rate in 146 games at second in his first season back.

Sandberg led the league in runs scored in 1984 (114), 1989 (104), and 1990 (116); total bases in 1990 (344); triples in 1984 (19); and home runs in 1990 (40).

One particular game in his MVP season, which came to be known as the "Sandberg Game" in Cubs lore, helped to launch him onto the national scene. On June 23, 1984, Sandberg went 5-for-6 with seven RBIs and two runs scored, including two late home runs in the extra-inning game, tying the game both times, before the Cubs eventually beat the Cardinals 12–11 in 11 innings.

I just remember as a kid the three home runs that were hit by Reggie Jackson in the World Series. That's a moment that kind of stands out. Another image that kind of stands out, that I saw as a kid and am reminded about, is George Brett running out of the dugout in the pine tar incident with Goose Gossage. So those are a couple of images that I remember and remember very clearly.

From my own career, the game I had against the St. Louis Cardinals on June 23, I hit two home runs off of Bruce Sutter. And that game was a game that a lot of people talk about. I ended up with five hits on the day and five or six or seven RBIs. And that game put the Cubs [near] first place for the first time in 1984, and then we held on for the rest of the year and then we went on to win the National League East.

It was always a big series, Cubs-Cardinals, and that day with national TV. The Cubs were toward the top of the standings for the first time in a lot of years. Winning that game kind of sent a message to all of us that, "Hey, we have a chance to do something here." And it really got the fans and the city of Chicago and in a lot of ways fans across the United States behind the Cubs. We took over first place about a week later and we kept it the rest of the year. So that game was seen across the nation, and did a lot for the organization, for the team that year, and for myself, getting me in my first All-Star Game. I received a lot of votes after that and took over first place. Going to the All-Star Game and then leading me to the National League MVP that year, that game had a lot to do with all those things.

I just remember the excitement that it created. The Cubs fans started to really come out and pull for the team. The city of Chicago really kind of took notice, "Hey, wait a minute, the Cubs are in first place. What's happening here?" So that game kind of got us going and jump-started us on our way to that season that we ended up having.

From that point on I hit Bruce pretty well, but not leading up to it. No, he was lights out. So that's what made it such a big deal, because he was such a devastating pitcher—that if guys even made contact, most of the time it was just ground balls because the ball just went down so hard. So I was able to lift two out of the stadium there at Wrigley for game-tying home runs, and it went on for 11 innings, and we ended up winning that game. Not only that, it was '84, I went on to an MVP year that year, and also that game got me into my first All-Star Game because, before that game, I was in second place behind Steve Sax of the Dodgers. After that game, I passed him. Because it was the Game of the Week, I got a lot of votes, and that got me into my first All-Star Game.

I think just for the fact that that was the season we ended up winning the pennant for the first time in a long time—and that was right in the middle of the season— a lot of the players said that was the game that really catapulted us to a whole 'nother level, saying, "Hey, we can do something here."

It's incredible. I'm sitting right here, and Bruce Sutter is right there, in the Hall of Fame. A lot of things have changed since then. So it's very cool. I remember it very well. We enjoyed it and we enjoy talking about it. I enjoy talking about it a little more than Bruce does. But it was a game that we both remember very clearly. And it was something that just happened.

Bruce Sutter

Howard Bruce Sutter
Born: January 8, 1953, in Lancaster, Pennsylvania
MLB debut: May 9, 1976
Final game: September 9, 1988
Teams: Chicago Cubs (1976–1980), St. Louis Cardinals
(1981–1984), Atlanta Braves (1985–1986, 1988)
Primary Position: Pitcher
Bats: Right—**Throws:** Right
Hall of Fame induction: 2006
Vote: 400 votes of 520 ballots cast, 76.92%

Originally chosen by the Washington Senators in the 21st round of the 1970 draft, Bruce Sutter elected not to sign, waiting until September 1971 to sign with the Cubs as a free agent. Although he spent the next four seasons in the minors before making his major-league debut, it was during that time that he learned from pitching coach Fred Martin how to throw the split-fingered fastball. The pitch would make Sutter one of the most dominant closers in baseball.

In his 12-season career, Sutter led the league in saves in 1979 (37), 1980 (28), 1981 (25), 1982 (36), and 1984 (45) and games finished in 1984 (63). His 45 saves in 1984 tied the major-league mark set by Dan Quisenberry the previous year.

He earned the National League Cy Young Award in 1979 with a record of 6–6, 37 saves, a 2.22 ERA, 110 strikeouts, and 32 walks (five intentional) in 101⅓ innings, becoming just the third reliever to win the award, after the Dodgers' Mike Marshall in 1974 and the Yankees' Sparky Lyle in 1977. He was also named both The Sporting News Fireman of the Year and Rolaids Relief Man of the Year in 1979, 1981, 1982, and 1984. A six-time All-Star, he appeared in four Midsummer Classics, earning wins in two and saves in the other two, without allowing a run in any of his appearances.

Sutter worked more than one inning in 188 of his 300 saves and pitched more than 100 innings in five seasons. He recorded 20 or more saves in nine consecutive seasons.

Upon retiring, he had amassed 300 saves, third most all-time, and compiled a record of 68–71, with a 2.83 ERA, 861 strikeouts against 309 walks, and 879 hits in $1042\frac{1}{3}$ innings, finishing 512 of the 661 games in which he appeared. He was the fourth reliever inducted into the Hall of Fame—with Hoyt Wilhelm, Rollie Fingers, and Dennis Eckersley—and the first pitcher who had never started a game.

With the Cubs facing the Cardinals on June 1, 1977, Sutter pitched five innings of the Cubs' 13-inning, 4–3 win, striking out nine. Later that season, against the Expos on September 8, he struck out six in three innings, pitching the last three frames and earning the *W* of the Cubs' 10-inning, 3–2 win. In the eighth and ninth innings, he struck out the side, including fanning the three batters he faced in the ninth on nine pitches, becoming the 12th NL pitcher (19th overall) to strike out the side on nine pitches.

Traded to St. Louis before the 1981 season, Sutter helped the Cards to the 1982 National League pennant, going 1–0 with a save in the three-game sweep of the Braves. In the World Series, he earned a win and two saves in four appearances, including Game 7, when he pitched the final two innings without allowing a hit. Sutter struck out the last batter he faced, Gorman Thomas, who had led the American League in home runs that season, to clinch the World Series for St. Louis.

———————————

I think if you talk to anybody, of course the first game that you're in the big leagues is special. But really, for me the most memorable game is the seventh game of the World Series in 1982.

We got close in '81, then we had the strike. I think we actually had the best record in the National League [East], but we didn't win either of the first half or the second half. So we didn't get in. But we knew we had a good ballclub. So in '82 we just knew that we were the best team, and we acted like it. We had a great manager. Whitey Herzog really made everybody a part of the team and treated the 25th player the same as he treated his No. 1 player, and he got everybody in, was smart on how to use guys, give guys days off, and was extremely smart with how he used the bullpen.

We went right down to the wire with the Phillies, trying to win the division title. And then we played Atlanta twice in St. Louis. We had the big crowds all season long, so we were used to it. Of course, St. Louis, they're sold out all the time. But when you're out in the field, you really don't hear it. It's kind of a buzz. You don't hear voices or anything; it's just kind of a loud buzz going. And after each pitch, everybody's reacting, the cheer goes up, and it's just an exciting time to play.

I remember Stuper pitched a good game in Game 6, and we had quite a few rain delays, and we ended up winning 13–1 or something. So it was going into Game 7, and I knew the game was going to come to me. I was going to throw the pitch that either won it or throw the pitch that lost it. I didn't pitch in Game 6, and Whitey had told me he wouldn't go to me before the sixth inning, but after the sixth inning it was going to be me if Joaquin got in trouble. So the whole day I was antsy. I was nervous. I was really, really excited to play that game, and of course the game came to me before the night was out.

When you're antsy like that, it can be tough to contain it. It's kind of funny, because I was a reliever, and everybody says you're always pitching with the game on the line. But I don't think I could have been a starting pitcher, knowing I was going to start the next day. And this was one of those games where I knew that I was going to pitch the next day. The other days it's kind of in doubt whether you're going to pitch or not. But for this one I knew that I was going to be in this game, and it was going to be on the line, and it was going to be the difference between winning a world championship and losing one. And it was going to come down to me. But, really, for relief pitchers, that's your job every day. But when it comes down to the seventh game, it really had me jacked up all day long. I couldn't wait to get to the ballpark and get the game started.

Joaquin was pitching a good game. We were winning 4–3, and Gantner made the last out in their seventh inning [grounding out to the pitcher], and they were close to first base. But they started mouthing back and forth, and they almost got in a fight, and then Whitey just looked at me and said, "You're the pitcher." So that's it, because Joaquin, he had a temper, and when he got mad, he never pitched better. So that was it for Joaquin. I came in and pitched the eighth inning, and we only have a one-run lead. Well, Milwaukee hit 200-something homers that year. Everybody in their lineup was a potential homer guy. You make one bad pitch, the game was tied. So I got through the eighth inning and nobody got on. We got done, and we scored two more runs in the bottom of the eighth. So that made my job a little bit easier, because now I had a three-run lead going into the ninth inning.

I hear guys talk about it today, when you can't hit a three-run homer with nobody on base. Back then some teams would take the first strike when they were down, and some teams wouldn't. Some teams would wait till the count got to 3–0, and then they would take a strike. That was one thing I always checked when we were playing teams: what did they do when they were two or three runs down? Because that was nice if they were going to give me strike one. And usually as a closer I had something to get strike three. They had one pitch to hit, and that was going to be it for them. And Milwaukee was a team that took the first-pitch strike. So then it was just a matter of throwing a get-me-over fastball first pitch and have strike one. So sometimes when teams would do that they actually would do me a favor. But Milwaukee had so many great hitters. Yount and Molitor both had 3,000 hits, and Simmons probably had 2,700. And there was Cecil Cooper; it just goes on and on. They had a great ballclub. So it was just a matter of throwing that first-pitch strike and try to get them to chase a second one.

It came down to we had over 200 steals and they had over 200 homers. We were playing in our park, which really helped us because our speed really came into play with defense. We had by far the best defensive team in baseball, I think, for two or three years. When you got Hernandez and Herr and Ozzie and Obie in the infield, and Lonnie and Willie and George in the outfield, and Darrell behind the plate, there weren't too many balls that fell in.

And we played in a big park. It was 414 to center and 386 to the alleys. Old Busch Stadium before they redid it was just a big, big ballpark.

After the last out, it was one of those things where I never showed emotion. My whole career, whether I won the game or lost the game. But that was one game where I kind of stuck my fist in the air then, and quickly I was on the bottom of the pile. Darrell was there first because I struck out the last guy, and then we met halfway between the pitcher's mound and home plate. Then it was just a matter of get up and get into the locker room, because everybody was coming, and it was just a free-for-all, and you didn't want to be on the ground.

It was two tough teams. We had our best starting pitcher, Joaquin, going, and we knew that he was going to keep us in the ballgame and that it was going to be a close game, that it was going to come down probably to the bullpens. And it did.

Tony Gwynn

Anthony Keith Gwynn
Born: May 9, 1960, in Los Angeles, California
MLB debut: July 19, 1982
Final game: October 7, 2001
Teams: San Diego Padres (1982–2001)
Primary Position: Right Field
Bats: Left—**Throws:** Left
Hall of Fame induction: 2007
Vote: 532 votes of 545 ballots cast, 97.61%

Starring in both basketball and baseball at San Diego State University, Tony Gwynn was selected in the third round of the 1981 draft by the San Diego Padres and in the 10th round by the NBA's San Diego Clippers the same year. Choosing baseball and the Padres, he went on to a 20-season career as one of the most consistent contact hitters in baseball history, becoming just the 17th player to spend an entire career of 20 or more seasons with one team, earning him the moniker "Mr. Padre."

Winning eight batting titles, tying Honus Wagner for the National League record, Gwynn hit over .300 every season except his rookie season—1982—when he hit .289. He went 2-for-4 in his big-league debut on July 19, 1982, against the Phillies, doubling for his first hit.

A 15-time All-Star, Gwynn earned seven Silver Slugger and five Gold Glove Awards. In the strike-shortened 1994 season he hit .394, the highest mark in baseball since Ted Williams' .406 in 1941.

Gwynn hit .338 with a .388 on-base percentage, 3,141 hits, 543 doubles, 85 triples, 135 home runs, 1,138 RBIs, 1,383 runs scored, and 319 stolen bases in 2,440 games in his career. With just 434 strikeouts, he fanned once every 21.4 at-bats.

He recorded a career-high six hits on August 4, 1993, against the Giants, going 6-for-7, and also had eight games throughout his career with five hits. He had a career-high five stolen bases on September 20, 1986, in Houston.

Gwynn led the league in batting in 1984 (.351), 1987 (.370), 1988 (.313), 1989 (.336), 1994 (.394), 1995 (.368), 1996 (.353), and 1997 (.372); on-base percentage in 1994 (.454); at-bats in 1986 (642); runs scored in 1986 (107); hits in 1984 (213), 1986 (211), 1987 (218), 1989 (203), 1994 (165), 1995 (197), and 1997 (220); singles in 1984 (177), 1986 (157), 1987 (162), 1989 (165), 1994 (117), 1995 (154), and 1997 (152); times on base in 1987 (303); sacrifice flies in 1997 (12); and at-bats-per-strike-outs in 1984 (26.3), 1989 (20.1), 1990 (24.9), 1991 (27.9), 1992 (32.5), 1994 (22.1), 1995 (35.7), 1996 (26.5), 1997 (21.1), and 1998 (25.6).

Now the head baseball coach at his alma mater, San Diego State, in 1999 he was ranked 49th on the list of Baseball's 100 Greatest Players compiled by *The Sporting News*.

Playing on the Padres' first three division champion teams, in 1984, 1996, and 1998, Gwynn led the Padres to their first NL pennant and World Series appearance in 1984, when they fell to the Tigers. In 1998 he helped the Padres to their second World Series appearance, where they fell to the

Yankees. In 27 postseason games, Gwynn hit .306, with a home run, 11 RBIs, and 11 runs scored. In two World Series, he hit .371, going 13-for 35 in nine games, with a home run, three RBIs, and three runs scored.

In his first game at Yankee Stadium, Game 1 of the 1998 World Series, he went 3-for-4, with a home run and two RBIs. But it's not his performance in the game that he remembers most.

My favorite game is Game 1 of the World Series in '98. And it doesn't have anything to do with the regular season or numbers. Playing at Yankee Stadium is my biggest thrill as a player, and having success in that game doesn't even compare to all the other stuff that happened there. Playing at Yankee Stadium, seeing the monuments, seeing the Hall of Fame guys, the retired numbers, Bob Sheppard calling my name, the whole thing. The whole experience for me was great. I had played 17 years in the big leagues and never had set foot in Yankee Stadium. I rode by it on a bus on plenty of occasions but never went in there. And running out to the line that night, wow, it was the best.

I was talking to Keith Olbermann in the dugout before the game, and he asked me about hearing my name announced. And I said just hearing [longtime Yankees PA announcer] Bob Sheppard call my name would be the coolest thing. And I didn't know he was standing right behind me, and I hear, *"Would you like it to be Anthony or Tony?"* And I almost fell off my chair. It was just awesome. So after the Series was over, Keith Olbermann sent me one of those little things where you push the button and you hear the recording, and on it Bob Sheppard was introducing my name. I put it in my trophy case. To me, that's part of Yankee Stadium. I actually didn't hear him announce me when I went out for the line, but I have that, and it will always be with me because that Game 1 was electric for me.

I wasn't nervous. It's tough enough being in the World Series, but that was a day I was really looking forward to. Forget the fact that we got swept in four games by possibly the best team ever to be put together. But it was awesome. It was awesome just being there.

Cal Ripken Jr.

Calvin Edwin Ripken Jr.
Born: August 24, 1960, in Havre de Grace, Maryland
MLB debut: August 10, 1981
Final game: October 6, 2001
Team: Baltimore Orioles (1981–2001)
Primary position: Shortstop
Bats: Right—**Throws:** Right
Hall of Fame induction: 2007
Vote: 537 votes of 545 ballots cast, 98.53%

Baseball's "Iron Man," Cal Ripken's streak of 2,632 consecutive games played, surpassing the mark of 2,130 straight games set by Lou Gehrig, will likely never be broken. The streak, which began May 30, 1982, in Baltimore's Memorial Stadium against the Blue Jays and ended more than 16 years later when Ripken sat out the September 20, 1998, game against the Yankees at Camden Yards, is just one of the highlights of Ripken's career.

Making his big-league debut as a 20-year-old with the Orioles on August 10, 1981, Ripken was named the American League Rookie of the Year the following season, homering in his first at-bat of the season, hitting .264 with 28 home runs and 93 RBIs, splitting time between shortstop and third base. In 1983 he was voted the AL MVP, hitting .318 with a .517 slugging percentage, 211 hits, 47 doubles, 27 home runs, 102 RBIs, and 121 runs scored.

He led Baltimore to the World Series title that season, as the O's beat the Phillies in five games. In 28 postseason games, he hit .336 with a home run, 10 doubles, eight RBIs, and 14 runs scored.

In 21 seasons, all with the O's, Ripken, one of baseball's most respected players, hit .276 with 3,184 hits, 603 doubles, 431 home runs, 1,647 runs scored, and 1,695 RBIs in 3,001 games.

He is one of just eight players in history with 400 home runs and 3,000 hits, joining Hank Aaron, Willie Mays, Eddie Murray, Stan Musial, Rafael Palmeiro, Dave Winfield, and Carl Yastrzemski.

A tall shortstop with power, Ripken redefined the way the position was played. In 1990 he set the record for fewest errors in a season at short, with three for a .996 fielding percentage. The next season he won the second of his MVP awards, hitting .323, slugging .566, with 210 hits, 46 doubles, 34 home runs, 114 RBIs, and 99 runs scored.

In 1987 the Ripken family made baseball history, as father Cal Ripken Sr. managed the O's, with Cal Jr. at short and brother Billy playing 58 games at second, the only time a father has managed two sons.

A 19-time All-Star, two-time All-Star Game MVP, two-time Gold Glove winner, and eight-time Silver Slugger winner, in 1999 Ripken was named to baseball's All-Century Team and was ranked 78th on the list of Baseball's 100 Greatest Players compiled by *The Sporting News*.

Ripken led the league in games played in 1983, 1984, 1987, 1989, 1991, 1992, 1993, and 1997 (all with 162) and in 1996 (163); at-bats in 1983 (663) and 1993 (641); plate appearances in 1983 (726); runs scored in 1983 (121); hits in 1983 (211); total bases in 1991 (368); doubles in 1983 (47);

extra-base hits in 1983 (76) and 1991 (85); and sacrifice flies in 1988 (10).

The night he broke Gehrig's record streak, September 6, 1995, in Baltimore against the Angels, was voted by fans as the most memorable moment in baseball history. For Ripken, though, with such a lengthy career and so many accomplishments, it is difficult to pick just one.

T hat's a tough one. I had a lot of interesting experiences. I might have to qualify my answer in a couple of different ways.

My favorite game from a human standpoint was probably the 2,131 game, because that lap—I was asked to take a lap around, which was the last thing I wanted to do—and it was an attempt to get the game started again because I felt bad that the game was being delayed on my account. I was pushed down the line and I started going through the motions of shaking hands and that sort of thing. And immediately it turned from a wonderful celebration of a packed house to a very intimate one-on-one. There were a lot of people that I recognized, some I knew their names, some I knew their faces. But it just became such a heartwarming experience to go all the way around the ballpark at that point in the game and it concluded with my little family in the front row. So I think that was my favorite game from a human standpoint. There were a lot of wonderful reactions from the fans. It couldn't be scripted. You couldn't even plan for something like that. The way that it unfolded, I remember feeling embarrassed. I just wanted to get the thing over with so we could start. But once the handshaking started, it became something to acknowledge. So I think that was probably, from a human standpoint, my favorite.

I would think there's a couple of games that stand out to me. When I was a young guy in the minor leagues, I hit three home runs in a game for the first time in my career, off the same pitcher on three different pitches. That was a game in Rochester. Doc Edwards was the manager. It was against the Indians affiliate. It must have been Charleston. The pitcher? Oh, shoot. A right-handed pitcher that threw fastballs, a pretty good curveball, and a slider. His name escapes me right now, but I'll remember. But that was symbolic for a couple of reasons. I got off to such a great start in Rochester. And you wonder, you're one step away from the big leagues, and you wonder if you have what it takes to make it. I remember that particular game it was just kind of a boost of confidence to me internally, to hit three home runs in a game, which I had never done anywhere. And having done that, it was like, "I think I'm going to make it." I got called up that year. It was 1981, after the strike was over. And that was the year I ended up playing in the 33-inning game in Pawtucket. That was one of the most interesting, bizarre games I ever played in because it was so cold, the wind was blowing straight in. It got called at 4:07 in the morning, and then we didn't resume it until June. It seemed like rosters had changed. The funniest part was after the game, at 4:07, we went to have breakfast at a Howard Johnson's. I remember going home for a little while and *Good Morning America* was on.

And the other one was kind of a personal moment with my dad. I couldn't tell you the exact moment in the game. But we were in Texas in the old ballpark [on August 20, 1982]. It was a tie game, and it went into extra innings. I had already established myself as a pretty good hitter. At that point, I got my feet on the ground. But I remember, I laid down a bunt to lead off the twelfth inning. I bunted for a base hit. And I was safe at first base, and ultimately I scored the winning run. And it was the acknowledgement from my dad that something as small as a bunt, when you're asked to hit home runs, and drive in runs, and I had hit for the cycle, and those kinds of things, but to have a bunt, and he said, "You really lifted the team. That was a big play in the game." He made a big deal out of it. So there's all kinds of great feelings you can get from the game.

I bunted off Steve Comer, who was a right-handed pitcher with a specialty change-up, a pitch that was particularly hard for right-handers to hit. I guess you already know when you have a walk-off homer everybody's celebrating at the plate. But I think in this case, somebody else knocked in the run, I scored it, somebody else saved the game, somebody else had a better game, because I don't think I hit very well in that game, because otherwise I wouldn't have been thinking about bunting! But those are the kind of heartwarming sort of moments that I reflect upon. I'm sure there's a million more of those.

The 2,131 game was very much like a fantasy, like it really wasn't happening to you. There're a few moments in your life when you kind of step outside your body and watch yourself. I remember that feeling with the birth of my two kids, being in the operating room, and feeling like everything was kind of closing in, kind of cloudy. When I was in that sort of celebration, you're trying to stay focused on what your training is supposed to be, and once the celebration started to occur, then it almost seems like you've stepped outside of your body, and just kind of watch everything. And then it just seemed like I was on autopilot.

I used to get asked about that game quite often, but not too much anymore. I always say that the two greatest

Cal Ripken tips his hat to the crowd in the middle of the fifth inning of the Orioles' September 6, 1995, game against the Angels. Ripken broke Lou Gehrig's record of 2,130 consecutive games in Baltimore's Oriole Park at Camden Yards.

baseball moments I've had I reference the 2,131 game as a human interaction sort of moment. I think the greatest baseball feeling is winning the World Series. I caught the last out of the [1983] World Series. The finality of that moment was very personal to me.

I think winning the World Series in particular is part of your childhood dream. I think we all as kids want to be baseball players or athletes, want to be the person that's celebrating winning the game, or to win the World Series by hitting a grand slam. I think everyone's played that. But then to actually live the dream by getting to play the game, period, and to be one of the ones to make it to the World Series. I think when you're a part of the World Series, it makes it more complete. It completes the dream.

Rich "Goose" Gossage

Richard Michael Gossage
Born: July 5, 1951, in Colorado Springs, Colorado
MLB debut: April 16, 1972
Final game: August 8, 1994
Teams: Chicago White Sox (1972–1976), Pittsburgh Pirates (1977), New York Yankees (1978–1983, 1989), San Diego Padres (1984–1987), Chicago Cubs (1988), San Francisco Giants (1989), Texas Rangers (1991), Oakland Athletics (1992–1993), Seattle Mariners (1994)
Primary position: Pitcher
Bats: Right—**Throws:** Right
Hall of Fame induction: 2008
Vote: 466 votes of 543 ballots cast, 85.8%

One of the most dominating and intimidating pitchers of his—or any—era, Rich "Goose" Gossage used a blazing fastball and fearless approach to become one of the most successful relievers in the game.

Selected by the White Sox out of Wasson High School in Colorado Springs in the ninth round of the 1970 draft, Goose made his major-league debut two years later, posting a record of 7–1 with two saves and a 4.28 ERA in 36 games, making one start.

In 22 seasons, Goose had a record of 124–107 with 310 saves, a 3.01 ERA, 1,502 strikeouts, and 732 walks in 1,809⅓ innings over 1,002 games. He started just 37 games, none after the 1976 season when he started 29 and threw complete games in 15. He recorded saves in 46 percent of the 681 games he finished.

Gossage recorded 20 or more saves in 10 seasons, leading the league in 1975 with 26, in 1978 with 27, and in 1980 with 33. In 1978 he also led the league in games finished with 55.

In four seasons with four different teams he logged 100 or more innings out of the bullpen, and pitched 224 innings as a starter in 1976. Goose earned 193 saves of four outs or more, and 52 saves of seven outs or more. In 19 postseason games, he posted a record of 2–1, with eight saves, and a 2.87 ERA, striking out 29, walking seven, and allowing 21 hits in 31 innings.

He helped his team to the postseason four times, winning three league pennants and a World Series championship with the Yankees in 1978. There, he appeared in three games and pitched six scoreless innings, giving up just one hit and one walk.

A nine-time All-Star, Goose earned the AL Rolaids Relief Man of the Year Award in 1978 and The Sporting News AL Fireman of the Year Award in 1975 and 1978. He is one of just five relievers inducted into the Hall of Fame—joining Hoyt Wilhelm, Rollie Fingers, Dennis Eckersley, and Bruce Sutter.

In 1978 he appeared in 63 games, posting a record of 10–11 with 27 saves and a 2.01 ERA in 134⅓ innings, with 122 strikeouts, 87 hits, and 59 walks, averaging more than two innings per appearance. But it was his final appearance of that season that is most memorable for him, in the Yankees' 163rd game of the season, facing the Red Sox in a one-game playoff at Fenway Park.

The 1978 playoff game was the biggest game for me. I pitched in a lot of big ballgames but none of that magnitude where you just play one game. We came down tied, with identical records. I think we flipped a coin and then we ended up going into Fenway and playing a one-game playoff. So it doesn't get any better than that, and especially the two teams, the Yankees and the Red Sox in Fenway Park. If there's one place you don't want to play one game, it's in Fenway Park, because no lead is really a safe lead. It's a difficult place to play.

It just stands out. Being a reliever, I pitched in a lot of tight situations and a lot of big games, playoffs, World Series games. But we ended up playing them and then obviously going on. We won the game and then we beat Kansas City and then we beat the Dodgers in the Series, and it was almost like spring training games after that game. The playoffs and the World Series were like exhibition games compared to that game. So that, by far, is the biggest game I ever played in.

It was just the magnitude of it, the whole setting really. That day it was just a beautiful fall, Indian summer, New England fall day. There was a little crispness in the air, and clear as a bell, and just a beautiful, gorgeous day. I'll just never forget it. It was quite a day and started out like that. I went to bed the night before thinking, "I'm going to be facing Yaz for the final out," and lo and behold that's what happened. I went to bed thinking that, and I don't know if it's in your subconscious mind, it actually plays out that way. But that was too weird.

I hadn't pitched particularly well all day really. I came in in a tight situation in the seventh with one out. Relieved

Guidry and got out of that jam, no harm, no damage. Then in the eighth inning I gave up a couple of runs to make it 5–4. When I came in, it was 5–2. Then the ninth rolls around and a couple guys get on. Piniella makes a great play in right field to save probably a tie ballgame, at least it would have been had somebody been on third, which they would have been. Then Rice hits the fly ball, which would have been a sacrifice fly. But now I'm standing on the mound. There's two outs. I think it was first and third, and here comes Yaz to the plate. And I've got a while to think about it. I sat there on the mound while he's getting a standing ovation, thinking, "Well, here's what you went to bed last night thinking, and here he is." But when I thought about it, I didn't think whether I got him out or not. I didn't get that far. I just knew I'd be facing him.

So I stood on the mound and I started talking to myself and I started asking questions and answering them. I first said, "Why are you so nervous?" And I've never been that nervous. We're always nervous, we just don't show it. So I just sat there and said, "Hey, why are you so nervous? You've always played the game for the love and the fun of it since you were eight years old. Why are you so nervous? What's the worst thing that can happen to me?" And I figured, "Well, I'll be back in Colorado tomorrow elk hunting."

And really it was the first time all day that I'd taken a deep breath and really collected myself. Before I was just trying to throw the ball instead of just staying within yourself and throwing like you can. You try to muscle everything and try to throw harder than you're capable of doing, and consequently the harder you try, the slower it goes. When I said, "What's the worst that could happen?" I didn't think, "Well, the season could end right here," because that's a negative thought. So I said, "The worst thing that could happen is I'll be home in Colorado tomorrow. It's not the end of the world," which I was bullshitting myself.

And then Yaz steps in. The first pitch is down. And it was really the first time all day that I had just taken a deep breath. Really, my legs were shaking. When I came into that game, I've never been so nervous in my whole life. Maybe the first time I pitched in the big leagues. That was no question the most nervous I ever was, absolutely. My legs, I didn't think I could get to the mound. My legs were shaking and trembling. I was trembling all over. I was nervous the whole time I was out there. It got better, but it was still off the charts. Then that first pitch to Yaz in that at-bat was down in the strike zone. I knew that was the hardest pitch I'd thrown all day. Then the next pitch was as hard as the first pitch, only the first one was down in the strike zone for a ball, then the next pitch was pretty much down the middle. And then he pops it up to Nettles.

When the ball went up, I'm watching it and I know it's going to stay in because he's camped under it. But most guys catch fly balls like this—they're under them and they catch them right in front of their face. Nettles catches balls like this [glove to the side of his head]. So I see this ball go by where I'm thinking it should be caught. And for an instant it was like, "Oh shit!" And then he ended up catching it. But for that split second it was like my heart jumped out, like damn! And then all hell broke loose. But it was a great day.

After the game, I'm in the training room just kind of gathering my thoughts and getting some ice and just having a beer and just kind of thinking, "Phew, I'm glad that's over with." It was pretty tiring. When you get that pumped up, it's a letdown, a big letdown, a good letdown. But it's very taxing. So I was sitting on the training table, and Munson comes in, and he goes, "Hey, where'd you get those pitches?" I said, "What do you mean?" He goes, "Those pitches had another foot on anything you'd thrown all day." So I said I finally relaxed. He goes, "What took you so damn long?"

But that's the biggest game I ever played in.

After that, we walked right through Kansas City and really walked right through the Dodgers. I think the whole second half we just kind of gradually built and kind of crescendoed at the end, finishing off everybody. That was a great ballclub. And the Red Sox had a great team. I kind of stood on the field that day and I remember thinking it's too bad there has to be a loser today because these are two great teams. It didn't seem fair that we would only play one game. It seemed like it should be a series, at least a five-game series. But it wasn't. It was only one game for everything.

Dick Williams

Richard Hirschfeld Williams
Born: May 7, 1929, in St. Louis, Missouri
MLB managerial debut: April 12, 1967
Final game: June 5, 1988
Teams: Boston Red Sox (1967–1969), Oakland Athletics
   (1971–1973), California Angels (1974–1976), Montreal
   Expos (1977–1981), San Diego Padres (1982–1985), Seattle
   Mariners (1986–1988)
Primary position: Manager
Hall of Fame induction: 2008
Vote: Elected to the Hall of Fame by the Veterans Committee

Dick Williams set the bar high in his rookie managerial season, establishing himself as a no-nonsense skipper who could turn underperforming teams into winners. His first challenge was the 1967 Red Sox, who had finished the previous season 72–90, 26 games back in ninth place in the 10-team league. Williams led the "Impossible Dream" Sox to first place with a 92–70 record in the American League, before falling to the Cardinals in seven games in the World Series. He was named Major League Manager of the Year by *The Sporting News* for his stellar rookie season.

Signed as a free agent by the Brooklyn Dodgers in 1947, Williams played 13 seasons with the Dodgers, Orioles, Indians, Kansas City Athletics, and Red Sox, batting .260 with 70 home runs and 331 RBIs in 1,023 games. He played first base, second, third, left field, center, and right. After retiring as a player in 1964 with Boston, he began managing the organization's Triple-A team in Toronto the following season, launching his managerial career.

Williams became just the second manager, with Bill McKechnie, to win pennants with three different teams. In 1972 and 1973 he led the Oakland A's to consecutive World Series championships, and in 1984 he won the National League pennant with San Diego, bringing the Padres to the World Series for the first time in franchise history.

In 21 seasons, Williams compiled a record of 1,571–1,451, a .520 winning percentage. He is currently 18th all-time in managerial wins. His teams posted 90 or more wins seven times, and he is the only manager to reach that mark with four different teams.

With more than 4,000 major-league games as both a player and a manager, it may be hard to pick just one. Still, the one that capped an improbable season is hard to forget.

Well, I could say one on the negative side. I sat on the bench in 1951 when Bobby Thomson hit the ball off Ralph Branca, the "Shot Heard 'Round the World" that got the Giants into the World Series. Beat us in a three-game playoff, then they played the Yankees in the World Series. That was my first year up. That was tremendous.

I had another thrill as a young rookie with the Dodgers. They played a charity game every year at Yankee Stadium, and this is 1951 also, prior to Branca's pitch to Thomson. We played the Yankees up there. It was a charity, a "milk-fund game" they called it. I replaced Duke Snider in center, and I ran out there real quick so I could pass Joe DiMaggio as he was coming in, and that was a big thrill, of course.

But it has to be the last game of the 1967 season when we beat Minnesota and we went to the World Series for the first time in 21 years. That was huge. I've been on a couple of World Series winners with Oakland. Both Series went seven games, against Cincinnati in '72 and against the Mets in 1973, and they were both thrilling. So I've had a number of thrilling games. I went 5-for-5 one time as a player, so that had to be thrilling.

But you have a lot of good peaks and valleys in the game, that you can remember. So I'd probably have to say the final game of 1967 that Lonborg pitched against Minnesota that put us in the World Series. That has to be huge. I'm a first-year rookie manager in the major leagues. That has to be a huge, huge thrill. I don't know of anything, even winning World Series, that I mention, that can top that final game in 1967 with Boston.

I was on the Brooklyn Dodgers when they won in 1952 and 1953, and the Yankees beat us in both World Series matchups. But I'm the manager in Boston and it's my first year, and I only had a one-year contract. So it meant I was going to work at least a couple more years. But that has to probably go down as one of the big things. They carried Lonborg off the field. The fans stormed the field, and by the time they got him to the clubhouse, he didn't have his sweatshirt. They ripped it out from underneath his jersey. They didn't harm him a bit. They just hugged him and did everything possible to protect him. And I know Yaz, in the month of September he hit well over .400, and in the last 12 games he hit over .500.

I wasn't nervous going into the game, no. Just excitement, ready to get going. We had to win the last two against Minnesota, and in both games, we were down 2–0 as late as the [sixth inning of the last game]. Luckily,

Jim Kaat came up with an elbow strain [in the first game]. He had to leave and we got the relievers. And then Dean Chance, who was quite a pitcher along with Kaat, he had us down 2–0, and we knocked him out and won both games. The club didn't quit. We were down eight runs one time against the Anaheim Angels and came back and won that ballgame. Everything happened in Fenway Park. Your lead was never safe. And it was a great environment as far as crazy things happening. And the fans were so appreciative. You couldn't get a seat the second half of the season there, or from then on until right now.

Sure has flown by. I've been on five other clubs, managed five other clubs since then, and it's been 20 years since I managed in the major leagues. So time has flown by. But you remember certain situations, and the people of New England. I was inducted into their Hall of Fame, the Red Sox Hall of Fame. They recalled everything, and that was just a few years ago. They recalled everything that went on in 1967, a lot of things that I didn't.

What I remember most is us turning a ballclub and an organization completely around. What is known now as Red Sox Nation is when that started. We were a 100-to-1 shot. I'm a rookie manager. [General manager] Dick O'Connell took a great chance in hiring me. I had to turn a country-club attitude into a winning attitude, and I knew the material was there, the players were there. They and the kids that came up with me from Toronto were going to help. Reggie Smith, and Mike Andrews, Russ Gibson, all those guys, Gary Waslewski, they all fit in and then they helped me a lot by letting the other players know how tough I was and how fair I was. But also I had played on that club just two years previously, or three years, 1964 was my last year. So I knew what went on, and it wasn't a good thing. I had a one-year contract. So if I was going down, I was going to go down my way. And it worked out well. Yaz was the big leader. Lonborg had an exceptional year. And, well, we swept all the awards. Yaz won the Triple Crown, the last time anyone has done that. He was the MVP. Lonborg was the Cy Young Award winner. Dick O'Connell was the executive of the year, and I got manager of the year. So it was a thrilling, thrilling first year for me as a major-league manager after having 13 years in the major leagues as a player.

I said in the spring and that was my only quote, "We'll win more than we lose." At the All-Star break, after Lonborg had military duty, pitched a game in Detroit, a second game, that we won, which stopped a four- or five-game losing streak. Right after that, we started on a 10-game winning streak that got us back in the hunt. Coming back, at the airport, we had to go to the other side of the tarmac so the bus could get us. The people swarmed the tarmac, and they had to shut down the airport till they got us safely over near the terminal. And that's when we knew we had the backing. And from that point on, we were sold out every night.

About the Author

M aureen Mullen is a freelance writer covering the Boston Red Sox and Major League Baseball. Her work appears in the *Boston Globe*, the *Lynn (Massachusetts) Daily Item*, MLB.com, and several other newspapers and websites. She also wrote *Diary of a Red Sox Season* with Red Sox legend Johnny Pesky.